AMONG FRIENDS

Mad about Muffins

A Cookbook for Muffin Lovers

RECIPES BY DOT VARTAN
ILLUSTRATIONS BY SHELLY REEVES SMITH

AMONG FRIENDS COLLECTION, INC.
LINN CREEK, MISSOURI

PUBLISHED BY AMONG FRIENDS, INC.

RR2 BOX 2121C, LINN CREEK, MISSOURI 65052

© 1996 BY AMONG FRIENDS

ACKNOWLEDGMENTS

Thank you Gentre for all your support in my first publishing venture.
Special thanks to my family and friends, especially Karen Vartan.

Vartan, Dot.
        Mad about muffins: recipes/by Dot Vartan;
Illustrated by Shelly Reeves Smith.
        p.   cm.
Includes Index.
Preassigned LCCN: 96-85410
ISBN: 0-9653117-1-6
1. Cookery. I. Smith, Shelly Reeves, III. II. Title

Printed in the United States of America

Last digit is the print number: 9 8 7 6 5 4 3 2 1

$\mathcal{P}$resented to:

I love muffins!

I used to buy a giant-sized bran muffin when I didn't have time to go out for lunch. I would quarter it, spread each quarter with butter, and eat it slowly while I worked at my desk. It would take me almost an hour to eat my bran muffin and I wouldn't need to eat anything else until dinner.

When the muffin shop closed permanently, I became very interested in baking muffins for myself. I did not find enough interesting recipes, so I decided to create a muffin cookbook. I enlisted the aid of my sister-in-law, Karen, and we made a list of about 100 muffin varieties to create recipes for. Of course, we had to include the standards, like blueberry and bran, but then we let our imaginations go wild with flavors such as apple brandy, cherry cheesecake, garlic corn, nectarine, lox and cream cheese, kiwi, Italian pizza, and zucchini.

It wasn't long before Karen and I started baking. We had our successes and our failures and we definitely had our share of eating muffins! After an afternoon of baking, we couldn't look at a muffin for a few days. Luckily, I had plenty of co-workers to help devour the samples. In fact, they came to rely on having me bring their muffin breakfast to the office.

Four years and sacks and sacks of flour later, I know a lot more about creating recipes from scratch, measurements, baking and cooking techniques, as well as proper recipe terminology. It has been quite a learning experience, and all I wanted was muffin recipes! Well, now I have them and would love to share them with you. I hope that you enjoy them!

BAKING PREPARATION

Most of my recipes can be prepared in about
15 minutes or less. The more complex recipes take
a few minutes longer, but are well worth the effort.
If your cupboard and refrigerator are stocked with
the basics like flour, sugar, baking powder, milk, and
butter, you can always whip up a batch of muffins.

The baking time listed is for a regular-size
muffin tin. Most recipes will also work well if
you use a mini-size or extra-large size muffin tin
as well. Generally, the mini size requires 10 to 15
minutes of baking time, while the extra-large size
requires 30 minutes or longer. Use a tester to
check if the muffins are done, but give them time
to rise by not opening the oven door during the
first few minutes of baking time.

The recipes call for butter, corn oil, whole milk,
and buttermilk as ingredients; however, you can
substitute your low-fat favorite, if you wish. I find
that using vegetable spray for greasing the tins
before baking works best. Let the muffins cool in
the pan for 10 to 15 minutes before removing them.

Have fun!

TABLE OF
CONTENTS

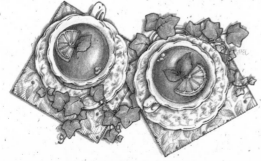

VARIATIONS ON A CAKE 79

FOR THE LITTLE ONES 91

Everyone's Favorites

Basic Muffins

2 cups minus 2 tablespoons sifted all-purpose flour
1 tablespoon baking powder
1/2 teaspoon salt
5 tablespoons granulated sugar
1 egg
1 cup milk
4 tablespoons melted butter

You can use this recipe as a base to add your own favorite ingredients!

Directions:

.Heat oven to 400°. In a large bowl, sift together the flour, baking powder, salt, and sugar. In another bowl, beat together the egg, milk, and melted butter. Pour the egg mixture into the flour mixture. Stir quickly and just enough to moisten the dry ingredients. Do not overmix - the batter will be lumpy. Fill greased muffin tins. Bake for 22 minutes or until the muffins are golden brown. Makes 10 muffins.

Cinnamon

3/4 cup softened butter
3/4 cup granulated sugar
1 teaspoon vanilla extract
2 eggs
1 3/4 cups all-purpose flour
1 teaspoon baking powder
1 teaspoon baking soda

Pinch of salt
1 cup sour cream

Topping:
1/2 cup chopped walnuts
3 teaspoons cinnamon
1/3 cup granulated sugar

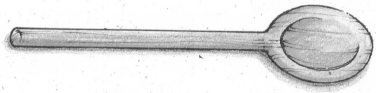

Directions:

Heat oven to 375°. In a large bowl, cream the butter and sugar with a mixer. Blend in the vanilla extract and eggs. In another bowl, sift together the flour, baking powder, baking soda, and salt. Pour the flour mixture and the sour cream into the butter mixture. Stir the batter by hand until the ingredients are blended. If batter is too dry, add a splash of milk.

Grease muffin tins. Prepare the topping by mixing together the walnuts, cinnamon, and sugar. Drop 1 tablespoon of batter into each muffin tin. Sprinkle with 1 teaspoon of topping. Top with 1 more tablespoon of batter. Sprinkle the tops with another teaspoon of topping. Bake for 15 to 20 minutes or until a tester comes out clean. Makes one dozen muffins.

Blueberry

6 tablespoons softened butter
2/3 cup granulated sugar
2 eggs
1 teaspoon vanilla extract
2 teaspoons baking powder
1/4 teaspoon salt
2 cups sifted all-purpose flour
1/2 cup milk
2 cups fresh or frozen blueberries

Streusel topping:

2 tablespoons butter
2 tablespoons brown sugar
1/4 teaspoon cinnamon
1/2 cup chopped walnuts

Directions:

Heat oven to 375°. In a large bowl, cream together the butter and sugar until fluffy. Beat in the eggs. Add the vanilla extract, baking powder, and salt. Mix in half of the flour and the milk alternately, mixing gently by hand. Then add the remaining flour and milk. Stir in the blueberries. Fill greased muffin tins or foil baking cups.

To make the streusel topping, cut the butter into small pieces and mix it with the brown sugar, cinnamon, and walnuts. Sprinkle the topping over batter. Bake 25-30 minutes until muffins are lightly browned. Makes one dozen muffins.

Refrigerator Bran

2 3/4 cups Nabisco 100% Bran™
15 ounces golden raisins
2 cups boiling water
2 cups granulated sugar
1 cup corn oil
1 cup molasses
1 quart 1% buttermilk

4 eggs
3 cups all-purpose flour
2 cups whole-wheat flour
1 teaspoon salt
5 teaspoons baking soda
3/4 teaspoon cinnamon
3 cups bran flakes

Directions:

Heat oven to 400°. Combine the 100% bran, raisins, and boiling water in an extra-large bowl. Stir in the sugar, corn oil, molasses, buttermilk, and eggs.

Sift together the all-purpose flour and whole-wheat flour, salt, soda, and cinnamon into a large bowl. Add the flour mixture to the buttermilk mixture and mix well. Stir in the bran flakes. Spoon the batter into greased muffin tins. Bake for 20 to 22 minutes or until a tester comes out clean. Makes 8 to 10 dozen muffins.

Bake these deliciously hearty muffins when you're expecting a crowd for brunch. The extra batter can be stored in the refrigerator for up to 2 months.

Boston Brown Bread

1/2 cup rye flour
1/2 cup yellow cornmeal
1/2 cup whole-wheat flour
3/4 teaspoon salt
1 1/2 teaspoons baking soda
1 egg

1/3 cup molasses
1/3 cup firmly packed
   dark brown sugar
1/3 cup corn oil
1 cup buttermilk
1 cup golden raisins

Directions:

Heat oven to 400°. In a large bowl, mix together the rye flour, cornmeal, whole-wheat flour, salt, and baking soda. In a small bowl, beat together the egg, molasses, brown sugar, oil, and buttermilk. Stir the egg mixture into the flour mixture and mix well. Stir in the raisins. The batter will be thin. Fill greased muffin tins to the top. Bake for 15 minutes or until a tester comes out clean. Serve hot. Makes one dozen muffins.

You will enjoy the taste of classic Boston Brown Bread in every mouthful. Serve these muffins warm loaded with butter!

Sweet Corn

1 1/4 cups all-purpose flour
3/4 cup yellow cornmeal
1/2 rounded teaspoon salt
1 tablespoon baking powder
1/3 cup granulated sugar
1 egg
1 cup milk
1/4 cup corn oil

Served warm and generously spread with butter these muffins will melt in your mouth!

Directions:

Heat oven to 400°. Combine the flour, cornmeal, salt, baking powder, and sugar in a large bowl. Lightly beat the egg in a small bowl. Add milk and oil to the egg and stir well. Pour the egg mixture into the flour mixture and blend the ingredients. Fill greased muffin tins. Bake for 20 to 22 minutes or until a tester comes out clean. Serve warm. Makes one dozen muffins.

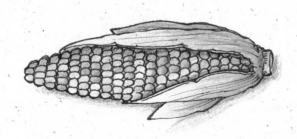

Dill

2 cups all-purpose flour
1 tablespoon granulated sugar
2 1/2 teaspoons baking powder
3 teaspoons dried dill weed
1/2 teaspoon salt
1/4 teaspoon ground pepper
1 large egg
1 cup (8-ounce container) small-curd
   cottage cheese
1/2 cup milk
4 tablespoons melted butter
1 tablespoon minced onion

Directions:

Heat oven to 400°. Sift the flour into a large bowl. Mix in the sugar, baking powder, dill weed, salt, and pepper.

In a medium bowl, beat the egg and stir in the cottage cheese, milk, melted butter, and minced onion with a whisk. Pour the egg mixture into the flour mixture and mix just until the dry ingredients are moistened. Fill greased muffin tins. Bake 15 to 20 minutes or until the muffins are lightly browned. Cool. Makes one dozen muffins.

Poppy Seed

3 cups all-purpose flour
2 1/4 cups granulated sugar
1 1/2 teaspoons baking powder
1 1/2 teaspoons salt
1 1/2 cups corn oil

1 1/2 cups milk
3 eggs
2 teaspoons almond extract
4 tablespoons poppy seeds

Directions:

Heat oven to 350°. In a large bowl, sift together the flour, sugar, baking powder, and salt. In another bowl, whisk together the corn oil, milk, eggs, and almond extract. Pour the milk mixture into the flour mixture and mix just until the dry ingredients are moistened. Stir in the poppy seeds. Fill greased muffin tins.

Bake for 30 minutes or until the muffins are golden brown. Serve warm or room temperature. Makes two dozen muffins.

Pumpkin

2 cups all-purpose flour
2 teaspoons baking powder
1 teaspoon ground cinnamon
1/2 teaspoon salt
1/4 teaspoon ground ginger
1/4 teaspoon ground nutmeg

1/8 teaspoon cloves
1/4 cup softened butter
1/2 cup granulated sugar
1 egg
1 cup canned pumpkin
1/2 cup evaporated milk
1/4 cup corn oil

Heat oven to 375°. In a medium bowl, sift together the flour, baking powder, cinnamon, salt, ginger, nutmeg, and cloves. In a large bowl, beat together the butter and sugar until they are creamy. Add the egg, pumpkin, evaporated milk, and corn oil. Beat on high speed until the mixture is light and fluffy. Add the flour mixture and stir just until the dry ingredients are moistened. Pour into greased muffin tins. Bake for 25 to 30 minutes or until tester comes out clean. Makes one dozen muffins.

A Garden Variety

Butternut Squash

1 cup cooked, puréed butternut
  squash
1/2 cup dark brown sugar
1/4 cup butter, softened
2 tablespoons molasses
1 egg

1 1/2 cups all-purpose flour
1 teaspoon baking powder
1/2 teaspoon baking soda
1/2 teaspoon salt
2 tablespoons orange juice

Directions:

Heat oven to 400°. Cut the squash into medium-sized chunks and put them into a glass cooking pan and cover with water. Microwave on high for 6 minutes or until squash is softened; then put the squash into a food processor or blender and purée. Set aside.

In a medium-sized bowl, cream the brown sugar, butter, and molasses with a mixer. Beat in the egg and the squash purée. In another bowl, sift together the flour, baking powder, baking soda, and salt. Stir the flour mixture into the squash mixture. Add the orange juice and stir just until the dry ingredients are moistened. Fill greased muffin tins. Bake for 15 to 20 minutes or until a tester comes out clean. Cool. Makes one dozen muffins.

Buttermilk Scallion

2 cups all-purpose flour
1 1/2 teaspoons baking power
1 1/2 teaspoons baking soda
1/2 teaspoon salt
2 tablespoons granulated sugar
1/2 cup chopped scallion

2 tablespoons butter
1 tablespoon white wine
  Worcestershire sauce
1 egg
1 cup lowfat buttermilk

Directions:

Heat oven to 375°. In a large bowl, sift together the flour, baking powder, baking soda, salt, and sugar. Sauté the chopped scallions lightly in butter and the white wine Worcestershire sauce.

In a medium bowl, lightly beat the egg. Mix in the scallion mixture and the buttermilk and stir this into the flour mixture until the dry ingredients are moistened. Fill greased muffin tins and bake for 15 minutes or until the muffins are golden brown. Makes one dozen muffins.

Carrot Pineapple

1 3/4 cups all-purpose flour
1 teaspoon baking powder
2 teaspoons baking soda
3/4 teaspoon cinnamon
1/2 cup dark brown sugar
1 egg
1/3 cup melted butter
1 (20 ounce) can crushed
    pineapple, drained

6 ounces pineapple juice (saved from
    the can of crushed pineapple)
1 cup shredded carrot

Cream cheese topping:
2 ounces cream cheese
1/4 cup sweetened condensed milk
2 teaspoons vanilla extract

Directions:

Heat oven to 375°. In a large bowl, sift together the flour, baking powder, baking soda, and cinnamon. Mix in the brown sugar. In another bowl, lightly beat the egg. Add the melted butter and pineapple juice. Mix in the crushed pineapple and shredded carrots. Pour the pineapple mixture into the flour mixture and mix by hand until the ingredients are blended.

Fill greased muffin tins. Bake 19 minutes or until the muffins are brown. Cool slightly and then remove the muffins from the tins.

While the muffins are baking, make the topping by blending the cream cheese, sweetened condensed milk, and vanilla extract. Spread the topping on the warm muffins. Makes one dozen muffins.

Vegetable Cheese

2 cups all-purpose flour
1 tablespoon baking powder
1/2 teaspoon salt
2 tablespoons granulated sugar
1 egg
1 cup milk
1/4 cup oil
2 tablespoons diced onion
3/4 cup grated sharp cheddar
    cheese
3/4 cup shredded zucchini
1/4 cup chopped green pepper
1/2 cup diced tomato

Directions:

Heat oven to 400°. In a large bowl, sift together the flour, baking powder, salt, and sugar. In another bowl, lightly beat the egg and stir in the milk and oil. In a third bowl, combine the onion, cheddar cheese, zucchini, green pepper, and tomato. Add the vegetables to the flour mixture and stir to coat well. Pour in the egg mixture and stir just until the dry ingredients are moistened. Fill the greased muffin tins. Bake for 20 minutes or until the muffins are golden brown. Makes one dozen muffins.

Zucchini Carrot

2 cups all-purpose flour
1/4 cup granulated sugar
1 tablespoon baking powder
1/4 teaspoon nutmeg
1/4 teaspoon cinnamon
1 cup shredded zucchini
1 cup shredded carrots
1 cup buttermilk
1/4 cup corn oil
2 eggs

Directions:

Heat oven to 400°. In a large bowl, sift together the flour, sugar, baking powder, nutmeg, and cinnamon. Mix in the zucchini and carrots. In a small bowl, combine the buttermilk, corn oil, and eggs. Add the buttermilk mixture to the flour mixture, stirring just until the dry ingredients are moistened. Fill greased muffin tins. Bake for 20 minutes or until the muffins are golden brown. Makes one dozen muffins.

Parsley Potato

1 1/2 cups all-purpose flour
2 tablespoons granulated sugar
1 tablespoon baking powder
1 teaspoon salt

1 egg
2/3 cup milk
1 1/2 cups mashed potatoes
1 tablespoon minced parsley

Directions:

Heat oven to 400°. In a large bowl, sift together the flour, sugar, baking powder, and salt. In a small bowl, beat together the egg and milk. In another bowl, mash the potatoes with the parsley. Stir the egg mixture into the flour mixture. Fold in the potatoes until the ingredients are blended. Fill greased muffin tins. Bake for 30 minutes or until the muffins are brown. Serve warm. Makes one dozen muffins.

Optional: Pierce the muffin tops with a tooth pick and drizzle with melted butter.

As a savory accompaniment to a steaming bowl of soup or your favorite stew, these hearty muffins cannot be surpassed.

Sweet Potato

2 cups sifted all-purpose flour
1 cup whole-wheat flour
4 teaspoons baking powder
1 teaspoon cinnamon
1/2 teaspoon nutmeg

1/4 teaspoon salt
3/4 cup light brown sugar
1 egg, lightly beaten
1/4 cup melted butter
1 cup milk
1 cup cooked, mashed sweet
   potato

Directions:

Heat oven to 375°. In a large bowl, mix the flours, baking powder, cinnamon, nutmeg, salt and 1/2 cup brown sugar. In another bowl, lightly beat the egg. Add the butter, milk, and sweet potato and combine well.

Pour the sweet potato mixture into the flour mixture and stir until the dry ingredients are blended. Fill greased muffin tins. Sprinkle the batter with the remaining brown sugar. Bake for 15 to 20 minutes or until a tester inserted into the center of a muffin comes out clean. Makes 18 muffins.

...A good recipe for leftover sweet potatoes from Thanksgiving dinner.

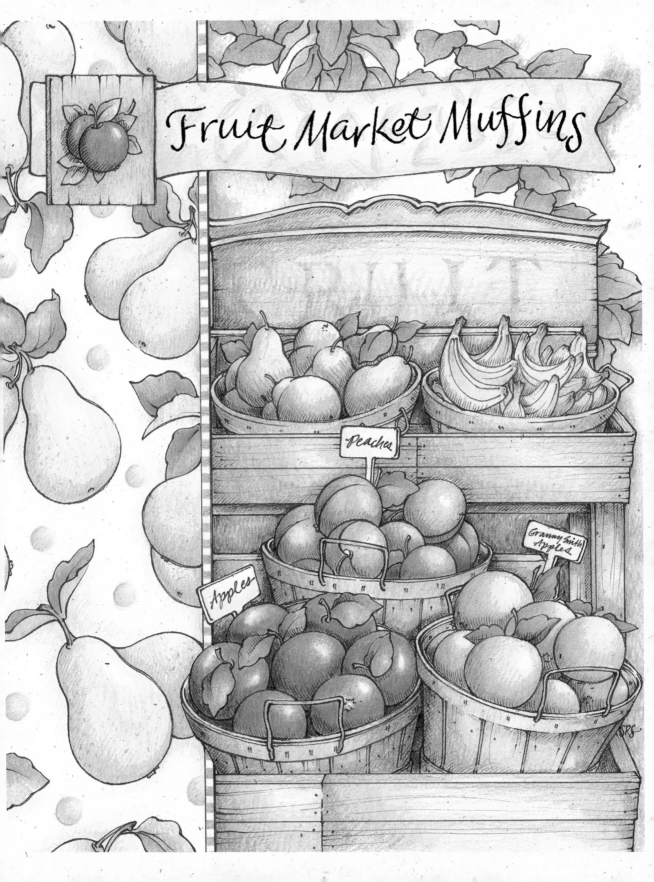

Fruit Market Muffins

Apple et Al.

Apples

2 teaspoons baking soda

2 teaspoons ground cinnamon

1/2 teaspoon salt

1/8 teaspoon ground nutmeg

1/4 cup toasted cracked wheat

2 cups carrots, peeled and
    finely shredded

1 large tart green apple, peeled,
    cored, and finely shredded

1/2 cup sliced and toasted
    almonds

1/2 cup shredded coconut

3 eggs

1/2 cup corn oil

2 teaspoons vanilla extract

1/2 cup raisins

1/2 cup apple juice

2 cups sifted all-purpose flour

1 cup granulated sugar

Directions:

   Heat oven to 350°. Soak raisins for 30 minutes in enough hot apple juice
to cover them and then drain off the apple juice, reserving it for later. In a
large mixing bowl, combine the flour, sugar, baking soda, cinnamon, salt,
nutmeg, and cracked wheat. Stir in the shredded carrots, shredded apple,
almonds, coconut, and drained raisins. In another bowl, beat the eggs with
the oil, vanilla extract, and apple juice. Add the egg mixture to the flour
mixture and stir just until combined.

   Spoon the batter into greased muffin tins. Bake for 20 to 22 minutes or
until the muffins are light brown. Serve them warm or at room temperature.
Makes about two dozen muffins.

Apple Squash

1 cup sifted all-purpose flour
1 cup whole-wheat flour
3 teaspoons baking powder
1 teaspoon cinnamon
1/2 teaspoon nutmeg
1/8 teaspoon cloves
1/4 teaspoon salt
1 cup grated Granny Smith apple

1 cup cooked and puréed squash
1/2 cup dark brown sugar
1 egg, lightly beaten
1/4 cup melted butter
1/3 cup buttermilk
1/2 cup apple juice

Directions:

Heat oven to 375°. Mix together the all-purpose flour, whole-wheat flour, baking powder, cinnamon, nutmeg, cloves, and salt into a large bowl.

Combine the apples, squash, brown sugar, egg, melted butter, buttermilk, and apple juice in a medium bowl. Stir the apple mixture into the flour mixture just until the ingredients are moistened.

Fill greased muffin tins. Bake for 20 minutes or until the muffins are browned. Makes 16 muffins.

Apricot Orange

2 1/4 cups all-purpose flour
1 tablespoon baking powder
1/4 teaspoon salt
1 teaspoon orange zest* (rind or peel)
1 1/3 cups canned apricots, coarsely
  chopped (save the juice)

1/2 cup granulated sugar
1/4 cup butter, melted
1/3 cup milk
1 egg, at room temperature
1/4 cup corn oil
1 teaspoon orange liqueur
  (optional)

Directions:

Heat oven to 400°. In a large bowl, sift together the flour, baking powder and salt. Stir in the orange zest and drained, chopped apricots, reserving the juice. Combine the sugar, butter, milk, egg, oil, 1/2 cup juice from the fruit, and orange liqueur in a medium bowl.

Make a well in the center of the dry ingredients. Add the butter mixture to the well and stir just until the dry ingredients are blended (the batter will be lumpy). Spoon the batter into greased muffin tins. Bake 20 minutes or until the muffins are brown and a tester inserted into the center comes out clean. Cool 5 minutes. Serve warm. Makes one dozen muffins.

*zest - use a zestor to remove the rind. It is a gadget with tiny holes that cut threads of zest when dragged across the rind.

Banana Mandarin

2 cups all-purpose flour
3 teaspoons baking powder
1/2 teaspoon salt
3 tablespoons granulated sugar
1 egg

3 tablespoons corn oil
1 (11 ounce) can mandarin
   oranges
1 large very ripe banana, slightly mashed
1 teaspoon orange zest (rind or peel)

Directions:

Heat oven to 375°. In a large bowl, sift together the flour, baking powder, salt, and sugar. In a medium bowl, beat together the egg and corn oil. Drain the oranges while saving the liquid in a measuring cup. Add enough milk so that the liquid measures one cup. Chop oranges into small pieces. Add the mashed banana and chopped oranges to the egg mixture.

Pour the reserved orange liquid and milk into the egg mixture along with the orange zest and blend well. Pour the egg mixture into the dry ingredients and stir together just until the ingredients are blended. Spoon the batter into greased muffin tins. Bake 20 to 25 minutes until the muffins are golden brown. Makes one dozen muffins.

Cherry Lemon

1 cup dried cherries
2 cups all-purpose flour
2 teaspoons baking powder
1 teaspoon baking soda
1/2 teaspoon salt
5 tablespoons granulated sugar

1 egg
1 cup buttermilk
5 tablespoons melted butter
Juice from one medium lemon
Lemon zest from one lemon
  (rind or peel)

Directions:

   Heat oven to 375°. In a food processor, chop the dried cherries (sprinkled with 2 tablespoons of the flour to separate them). In a large bowl, sift together the flour, baking powder, baking soda, salt, and sugar.

   In another bowl, lightly beat the egg. Add the buttermilk, melted butter, lemon juice, and lemon zest and combine well. Add the chopped cherries. Stir the buttermilk mixture into the flour mixture just until the dry ingredients are moistened. Pour into greased muffin tins. Bake 20 minutes or until the muffins are brown. Makes one dozen muffins.

   The tart taste of cherry creates an elegant muffin to serve at teatime. Dried cherries are available at health-food stores.

Cherry Yogurt

1/2 cup softened butter
3/4 cup granulated sugar
2 large eggs
1 teaspoon baking powder
1/2 teaspoon baking soda

1 teaspoon almond extract
2 cups sifted all-purpose flour
1 cup plain yogurt
1 (12 ounce) can cherry pie
   filling
1/2 cup pecan halves

Directions:

Heat oven to 350°. In a large bowl, beat butter with a mixer until creamy. Beat in sugar until the mixture is pale and fluffy. Beat in the eggs, one at a time. Mix in the baking powder, baking soda, and almond extract. Fold in half of the flour with a spatula; then add the yogurt and the remaining flour.

Line muffin tins with paper baking cups. Spoon one heaping tablespoon of batter into each cup and smooth the batter to distribute it evenly. Add 1 teaspoon of cherry pie filling to each cup. Cover the filling with another heaping tablespoon of batter. Break pecan halves and sprinkle on top of the batter. Bake 25 minutes or until the muffins are lightly browned. Makes one dozen muffins.

Coconut

1 2/3 cups all-purpose flour
1/4 cup granulated sugar
2 teaspoons baking powder
1/2 teaspoon salt
1/2 cup plus 2 tablespoons
    sliced almonds
1 cup plus 2 tablespoons
    coconut

1/2 cup raisins
1/2 cup chopped dates
1 egg
1/2 cup milk
1/4 cup plus 2 teaspoons
    firmly packed brown sugar
5 tablespoons melted butter
1/4 teaspoon cinnamon

Directions:

Heat oven to 375°. In a large bowl, sift together the flour, granulated sugar, baking powder, and salt. Stir in the 1/2 cup almonds, 1 cup coconut, the raisins, and the dates. In another bowl, beat the egg, milk, 1/4 cup brown sugar, and 3 tablespoons melted butter. Stir the egg mixture into the flour mixture just until the dry ingredients are moistened.

Spoon the batter into greased muffin tins. Sprinkle with a mixture consisting of 2 tablespoons almonds, 2 tablespoons coconut, 2 tablespoons melted butter, 2 teaspoons brown sugar, and 1/4 teaspoon cinnamon that has been blended. Bake for 25 minutes or until a tester comes out clean. Makes one dozen muffins.

Ginger Pumpkin

2 cups sifted all-purpose flour
1/2 cup packed light brown sugar
2 teaspoons baking powder
2 teaspoons ground cinnamon
1/2 teaspoon baking soda
1 cup canned pumpkin
1/2 cup molasses
2 eggs
1/3 cup softened butter
1/4 cup milk
1 teaspoon ground ginger

Directions:

Heat oven to 350°. In a large bowl, combine 1 cup flour, the brown sugar, baking powder, cinnamon, and baking soda. Add the pumpkin, molasses, eggs, butter, milk, and ginger. Beat with a hand mixer until the ingredients are combined. Add the remaining cup of flour and stir until it is blended. Fill greased muffin tins full. Bake for 20 to 25 minutes or until a tester inserted into a muffin comes out clean. Cool. Makes one dozen muffins.

Pumpkin Apple

2 cups all-purpose flour
1 1/2 cups granulated sugar
1 teaspoon baking soda
1 teaspoon baking powder
1/2 teaspoon salt
1 tablespoon pumpkin pie spice
1 egg, lightly beaten
1 cup canned pumpkin
1/2 cup evaporated milk
1/3 cup corn oil
1 cup peeled, finely chopped
   apples

Topping
2 tablespoons all-purpose flour
1/4 cup granulated sugar
1/2 teaspoon cinnamon
4 teaspoons butter
1/4 cup finely chopped walnuts

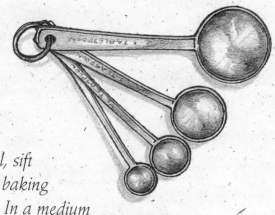

Directions:

Heat oven to 350°. In a large bowl, sift together the flour, sugar, baking soda, baking powder, salt, and pumpkin pie spice. In a medium bowl, combine the egg, pumpkin, evaporated milk, and corn oil. Add the egg mixture to the flour mixture and stir just until the dry ingredients are moistened. Stir in the apples. Spoon the batter into greased muffin tins.

To make the topping, combine the 2 tablespoons of flour, 1/4 cup sugar, and 1/2 teaspoon ground cinnamon in a small bowl. Cut in 4 teaspoons butter until the mixture is crumbly. Stir in the chopped walnuts. Sprinkle the streusel topping over the batter. Bake for 35 to 40 minutes or until a tester inserted into a muffin comes out clean. Makes 18 muffins.

The subtle spices of pumpkin pie blends with the moistness of apple cake in this marvelous creation with its delicious crunchy topping.

Orange Pineapple

1 1/2 cups all-purpose flour
1/4 cup dark brown sugar
2 teaspoons baking powder
1/4 teaspoon salt
2 eggs
1/2 cup orange juice
1/4 cup melted butter
1 (8 ounce) can crushed pineapple

Marmalade glaze
1/4 cup orange marmalade
1 tablespoon water

Directions:

Heat oven to 375°. In a large mixing bowl, stir together the flour, dark brown sugar, baking powder, and salt. In a small bowl, beat the eggs. Stir in orange juice and melted butter. Drain the crushed pineapple. Combine the pineapple with the egg mixture. Add the egg mixture to the flour mixture. Mix until the ingredients are completely blended.

Spoon the batter into greased muffin tins. Bake for 18 minutes or until a tester inserted into a muffin comes out clean. Remove the muffins from the oven.

With a toothpick, poke holes in the tops of the muffins. Make the marmalade glaze by mixing together the marmalade and the water. Spread 1 teaspoon glaze over the tops of the muffins. Makes one dozen muffins.

New England Banana

1 3/4 cups all-purpose flour
1 teaspoon baking soda
1/2 teaspoon baking powder
1/2 cup granulated sugar
1/4 cup melted butter

1 egg, slightly beaten
1 teaspoon vanilla extract
2 medium bananas, mashed
4 tablespoons milk
4 tablespoons maple syrup

Directions:

Heat oven to 375°. In a medium bowl, sift together the flour, baking soda, and baking powder. Mix in the sugar.

In a large bowl, combine the melted butter, beaten egg, vanilla extract, bananas, milk, and maple syrup and beat with a fork until well blended. Stir the banana mixture into the flour mixture, just until the dry ingredients are moistened. Spoon the batter into greased muffin tins. Bake 20 minutes or until the muffins are lightly browned. Serve warm. Makes one dozen muffins.

Seasonal Fruits

Blueberry Orange

2 cups all-purpose flour
1 tablespoon baking powder
1/2 teaspoon baking soda
1/2 teaspoon salt
1/4 cup brown sugar, firmly packed
6 ounces orange yogurt

1/3 cup orange juice
2 tablespoons melted butter
2 tablespoons corn oil
1 egg, beaten
Zest from one orange (rind or peel)
1 cup fresh or frozen blueberries

Directions:

Heat oven to 375°. In a large bowl, sift together the flour, baking powder, baking soda, and salt. Stir in the brown sugar. In a medium-sized bowl, combine the orange yogurt, orange juice, melted butter, corn oil, egg, and orange zest.

Pour the yogurt mixture into the flour mixture and mix until the dry ingredients are moistened. Gently stir in the blueberries. Fill greased muffin tins full. Bake 20 minutes or until muffins are golden brown. Serve warm. Makes one dozen muffins.

Banana Strawberry

3/4 cup butter, at room temperature
2/3 cup firmly packed light brown
   sugar
3 ripe bananas
2 eggs
1 cup cake flour
1 cup all-purpose flour
3/4 teaspoon salt
1 1/2 teaspoons baking soda
1 teaspoon baking powder
1 cup sliced fresh strawberries
2 tablespoons granulated sugar

Note: It is important that fresh strawberries be used, because frozen strawberries are too soggy.

Directions:

Heat oven to 375°. In a large bowl, cream the butter. Add the sugar and blend well. Purée the bananas in a food processor. Stir the puréed bananas and eggs into the butter mixture, beating until the batter is smooth.

In a medium bowl, sift together the cake flour, all-purpose flour, salt, baking soda, and baking powder. Add the flour mixture to the batter and mix well. Stir in the sliced strawberries. Spoon the batter into greased muffin tins or into foil baking cups. Sprinkle the tops with granulated sugar. Bake 20 minutes. Serve warm. Makes one dozen muffins.

Cranberry Apple

2 cups minus 2 tablespoons
   all-purpose flour
1 tablespoon baking powder
2 tablespoons granulated sugar
1/2 teaspoon salt
1 egg
1/4 cup apple juice

3/4 cup milk
4 tablespoons melted butter
1 cup chopped fresh cranberries
1 medium apple, chopped
1/2 cup chopped walnuts

Directions:

   Heat oven to 375°. In a large bowl, sift together the flour, baking powder, sugar, and salt. In another bowl, lightly beat the egg. Add the apple juice, milk, melted butter, chopped cranberries, chopped apple, and chopped walnuts. Mix well. Pour the egg mixture into the flour mixture and stir just until the dry ingredients are moistened. Pour the batter into greased muffin tins. Bake 22 minutes or until the muffins are brown. Makes one dozen muffins.

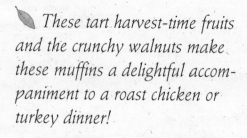

   These tart harvest-time fruits and the crunchy walnuts make these muffins a delightful accompaniment to a roast chicken or turkey dinner!

34

Cranberry Hazelnut

1 1/2 cups all-purpose flour
1 teaspoon ground cinnamon
1/2 teaspoon baking powder
1/4 teaspoon baking soda
1/4 teaspoon ground cloves
1 cup fresh cranberries
1/3 cup golden raisins
1/3 cup hazelnuts
2 eggs
3/4 cup packed light
   brown sugar
1/2 cup orange juice
1/3 cup corn oil
1 teaspoon brandy

Directions:

Heat oven to 350°. In a large bowl, sift together the flour, cinnamon, baking powder, baking soda, and cloves. In a food processor, finely chop the cranberries, raisins, and hazelnuts. In a medium bowl, beat the eggs. Stir in the brown sugar, orange juice, corn oil, and brandy. Mix the chopped cranberries, raisins, and hazelnuts and then pour the egg mixture into the flour mixture. Stir well. Fill the greased muffin tins. Bake for 20 minutes. Makes one dozen muffins.

Cranberry Orange

2 cups minus 2 tablespoons
  all-purpose flour
1 tablespoon baking powder
1/2 teaspoon salt
1 egg
1/4 cup light brown sugar

1 cup milk
2 tablespoons frozen orange juice
  concentrate
4 tablespoons melted butter
2/3 cup orange marmalade
1 1/2 cups whole fresh cranberries

Directions:

  Heat the oven to 375°. In a large bowl, sift together the flour, baking powder, and salt. In another bowl, lightly beat the egg. Add to this the brown sugar, milk, orange juice concentrate, melted butter, and marmalade. Mix well. Stir the orange juice mixture and the cranberries into the flour mixture just until blended. Fill greased muffin tins. Bake for 20 minutes or until the muffins are lightly browned. Makes one dozen muffins.

Note: Remember that fresh cranberries are only available from September to December!

36

Cranberry Pineapple

1 cup whole fresh cranberries
1 egg
1/2 cup milk
1/4 cup melted butter
1/2 cup drained crushed pineapple
1 1/2 cups all-purpose flour

2/3 cup granulated sugar
2 teaspoons baking powder
3/4 teaspoon salt
1/2 teaspoon cinnamon
1/2 teaspoon nutmeg
1/4 cup brown sugar

Directions:

   Heat oven to 375°. In a large bowl, combine the cranberries, egg, milk, butter, and pineapple. In another bowl, sift together the flour, granulated sugar, baking powder, salt, cinnamon, and nutmeg. Stir the flour mixture into the egg mixture just until moistened. Spoon batter into greased muffin tins. Sprinkle with brown sugar. Bake for 20 to 25 minutes or until the muffins are brown. Makes one dozen muffins.

 Tropical pineapple and tart cranberries--a wonderful taste sensation!

Nectarine Blueberry

1 1/2 cups all-purpose flour
2 teaspoons baking powder
1/4 teaspoon baking soda
1/4 teaspoon salt
3/4 cup granulated sugar
1/2 teaspoon allspice
1/3 cup softened butter
1 teaspoon orange zest (rind or peel)
1/4 cup orange juice
2 eggs
2 medium nectarines, peeled and
  coarsely chopped
1/2 cup fresh blueberries
2/3 cup chopped almonds
1 tablespoon granulated sugar

Directions:

Heat oven to 350°. In a large bowl, sift together the flour, baking powder, baking soda; and salt. Add the sugar, allspice, butter, orange zest, orange juice, and eggs. Beat with a mixer until ingredients are blended. Carefully fold in the chopped nectarines, blueberries, and 1/4 cup chopped almonds.

Fill greased muffin tins. Stir together 1 tablespoon sugar and the remainder of the almonds. Sprinkle on top of the batter. Bake for 20 minutes or until the muffin tops are lightly browned. Serve warm. Makes one dozen muffins.

Pear Cardamom

2 overripe pears
4 teaspoons lemon juice
2 cups all-purpose flour
1 tablespoon baking powder
1/4 teaspoon salt
1/2 cup granulated sugar
1 egg
1/2 cup melted butter
1 (6 ounce) can pear nectar
1/2 teaspoon cardamom

Cardamom infuses an exotic sweetness to the succulent fruit in these beguiling little cakes.

Directions:
   Heat oven to 375°. Chop the pears and soak the pieces in lemon juice in a small bowl. In a large bowl, sift together the flour, baking powder, salt, and sugar. In another bowl, lightly beat the egg and add the melted butter. Stir in the pear nectar and cardamom.
Pour the egg mixture into the dry ingredients and stir just until the flour mixture is moistened. Strain the lemon juice from the pears and fold in the pears into the batter. Fill greased muffin tins. Bake for 25 minutes or until the muffins are lightly browned. Makes one dozen muffins.

Plum

3 purple plums
1 1/4 cups all-purpose flour
1/2 teaspoon salt
1/2 cup granulated sugar
1 tablespoon baking powder
1/2 teaspoon cinnamon
1/2 cup softened butter
2 teaspoons fresh lemon juice
2 eggs

Topping
1/2 teaspoon cinnamon
2 tablespoons granulated sugar

Directions:

Heat oven to 375°. Remove the pits from the plums and slice the fruit into 1/4 in. thick rounds. In a large bowl, sift together the flour, salt, sugar, baking powder, and cinnamon. In a small bowl, beat together the butter, lemon juice, and eggs.

Pour the egg mixture into the flour mixture and blend. Drop 1 table-spoon of batter into greased muffin tins. Place a slice of plum on top. Cover with 1 more tablespoon of batter. Sprinkle with a topping made by combining 1/2 teaspoon of cinnamon and 2 tablespoons of sugar. Bake for 15 to 20 minutes or until a tester inserted into a muffin comes out clean. Makes 10 muffins.

Fresh Raspberry

2 1/2 tablespoons butter
1/2 cup granulated sugar
1 1/2 cups sifted all-purpose flour
1 1/4 teaspoons baking powder
1/2 teaspoon salt
1 egg
1/2 cup half and half
1 cup fresh raspberries

Directions:

Heat oven to 350°. In a large bowl, cream butter and sugar. Mix in the flour, baking powder, and salt. In a small bowl, lightly beat the egg. Stir in the half and half. Combine the egg mixture with the flour mixture and stir just until the dry ingredients are moistened.

Grease 6 to 7 muffin tins. Fill each with 1 tablespoon of batter. Place 4 to 5 raspberries on the batter and then add 1 more tablespoon of batter. Bake for 18 minutes or until the muffins are golden brown. While they are still hot, sprinkle the tops with granulated sugar. Let the muffins cool in the tins for 6 to 8 minutes before removing. Makes one-half dozen muffins.

Raspberry Apple

1/2 cup firmly packed dark brown
    sugar
3 tablespoons corn oil
1 egg
1/2 cup all-purpose flour
1/2 cup cake flour
1 teaspoon baking powder
1/2 teaspoon baking soda

1/2 teaspoon cinnamon
    Pinch salt
1 large Granny Smith apple
    (peeled and chopped)
1 cup fresh or frozen
    raspberries without syrup
    (do not thaw frozen
    raspberries)

Directions:

    Heat oven to 350°. In a large bowl, beat together the brown sugar, corn oil, and egg. In another bowl, sift together the flours, baking powder, baking soda, cinnamon, and salt.

    Add the flour mixture to the egg mixture and mix lightly. Carefully fold the raspberries and apples. Fill greased muffin tins. Bake for 28 to 30 minutes or until the muffins are lightly browned. Cool 10 minutes before removing the muffins from the tins. Serve warm. Makes one dozen muffins.

Raspberry Lemon

2 cups all-purpose flour
1 cup granulated sugar
3 teaspoons baking powder
1/2 teaspoon salt
1 cup half and half

1/2 cup corn oil
1 teaspoon lemon extract
2 eggs
1 cup fresh or frozen raspberries without syrup (do not thaw frozen raspberries)

Directions:

Heat oven to 425°. In a large bowl, sift together the flour, sugar, baking powder, and salt. In another bowl, combine the half and half, corn oil, lemon extract, and eggs. Blend well.

Add the half and half mixture to the dry ingredients and mix just until the ingredients are combined. Carefully fold in the raspberries. Fill greased muffin tins. Bake for 20 minutes or until the muffins are lightly browned. Cool. Makes one dozen muffins.

These muffins will be a hit at your next luncheon.

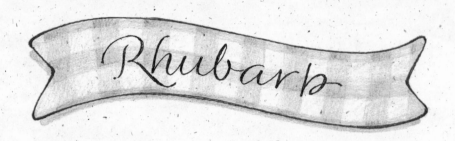

Rhubarb

2 cups all-purpose flour
1 tablespoon baking powder
1/4 teaspoon salt
1/4 teaspoon ground
  cinnamon
1 egg
1/2 cup light brown sugar

3 tablespoons strawberry jelly
1 cup milk
4 tablespoons melted butter
1 teaspoon vanilla extract
1 1/2 cups finely diced
  fresh rhubarb

Directions:

Heat oven to 375°. In a large bowl, sift together the flour, baking powder, salt, and cinnamon. In another bowl, lightly beat together the egg, brown sugar, and strawberry jelly. Stir in the milk, butter, and vanilla extract. Add the finely diced rhubarb. Pour the rhubarb mixture into the dry ingredients. Mix just until the ingredients are combined. Fill the greased muffin tins. Bake for 25 to 30 minutes or until the muffins are lightly browned. Cool. Makes 14 muffins.

Those With Nuts

Brazil Nut

2 cups all-purpose flour
2/3 cup firmly packed
   light brown sugar
2 teaspoons baking powder
1/2 teaspoon salt
1 cup dried apricots

3/4 cup boiling water
1/2 cup corn oil
1 egg, lightly beaten
1 teaspoon vanilla
1 cup coarsely chopped
   Brazil nuts

Directions:

Heat oven to 350°. In a large bowl, stir together the flour, brown sugar, baking powder, and salt. In another bowl, combine apricots with boiling water. Let stand 5 minutes. Stir in the oil, apricot, egg and vanilla until blended. Make a well in the center of the dry ingredients. Add the apricot mixture and stir just to combine. Stir in the nuts. Fill greased muffin tins. Bake for 20 minutes or until a tester comes out clean. Cool. Makes one dozen muffins.

Cashew

3/4 cup corn oil
1 cup sugar
2 eggs
1/2 cup milk
1 teaspoon vanilla
2 cups all-purpose flour

3/4 teaspoon baking soda
1/2 teaspoon salt
3/4 teaspoon ground cinnamon
1/4 teaspoon allspice
1 1/2 cups lightly salted
    cashews, chopped

1 cup white chocolate morsels

Directions:

Heat oven to 350°. In a large bowl, beat the oil and sugar with a mixer until creamy. Add the eggs, milk, and vanilla and beat for 1 minute. In another bowl, stir together the flour, baking soda, salt, cinnamon, and allspice. Add the dry ingredients to the oil mixture. Stir just to combine. Stir in the cashews and white chocolate morsels. Fill greased muffin tins. Bake for 20 minutes or until a tester comes out clean. Cool. Makes one dozen muffins.

Macadamia Nut

2 cups all-purpose flour
1/3 cup sugar
2 teaspoons baking powder
1/4 teaspoon salt
1 cup chopped macadamia nuts
2/3 cup coconut

1/2 cup chopped dried pineapple
3/4 cup milk
1/2 cup butter, melted
1 egg, lightly beaten
1 teaspoon vanilla

Directions:

Heat oven to 350°. In a large bowl, stir together the flour, sugar, baking powder, and salt. Stir in the nuts, coconut, and pineapple to coat. In another bowl, blend together the milk, butter, egg and vanilla. Make a well in the center of the dry ingredients. Add the milk mixture and stir just to combine. Fill greased muffin tins. Bake 18 to 20 minutes, or until a tester comes out clean. Cool. Makes one dozen muffins.

Peanut

2 cups all-purpose flour
2 teaspoons baking powder
1/2 teaspoon salt
1/2 cup firmly packed light-brown
   sugar
1/2 cup butter, melted

3/4 cup milk
1 egg, lightly beaten
1 teaspoon vanilla
1 cup peanut butter chips
1 cup finely chopped peanuts

Directions:

Heat oven to 350°. In a large bowl, stir together the flour, baking powder, and salt. In another bowl, blend together the brown sugar, butter, milk, egg and vanilla. Make a well in the center of the dry ingredients. Add the milk mixture and stir just to combine. Stir in the chips and the peanuts. Fill greased muffin tins. Bake 18 to 20 minutes, or until a tester comes out clean. Cool. Makes one dozen muffins.

Chunky Pecan

1 3/4 cups coarsely broken
   pecans
1 1/2 cups all-purpose flour
2 teaspoons baking powder
1/4 teaspoon salt
1/8 teaspoon allspice
1/2 cup firmly packed
   light brown sugar
1/2 cup melted butter
1/3 cup milk
1/4 cup maple syrup
1 egg
1 teaspoon vanilla extract

Topping
1/4 cup coarsely broken pecans
2 tablespoons light brown sugar

Directions:

   Heat oven to 375°. Toast the pecans in the oven for 10 minutes. In a large bowl, sift together the flour, baking powder, salt, and allspice. Stir in 1 3/4 cups of the toasted pecans. In a medium bowl, whisk together 1/2 cup brown sugar, butter, milk, maple syrup, egg, and vanilla extract.

   Make a well in the center of the dry ingredients and add the butter mixture. Stir just until blended. Fill greased muffin tins. Sprinkle with a topping made by mixing together two tablespoons brown sugar and the remainder of the toasted pecans. Bake for 20 minutes or until a tester inserted into a muffin comes out clean. Serve warm. Makes one dozen muffins.

Pine Nut

2 cups all-purpose flour
1/4 cup sugar
1 teaspoon baking soda
1/4 teaspoon salt
1 cup plain yogurt
3/4 cup milk

1/4 cup butter, melted
1 egg, lightly beaten
2 tablespoons honey
1 teaspoon vanilla
1 cup chopped dried apricots
3/4 cup pine nuts

Directions:

Heat oven to 400°. In a large bowl, stir together the flour, sugar, baking soda, and salt. In another bowl, stir together the yogurt, milk, butter, egg, honey, and vanilla until blended. Make a well in the center of the dry ingredients. Add the yogurt mixture and stir just to combine. Stir in the apricots and all but 2 tablespoons of the pine nuts. Fill greased muffin tins and sprinkle batter with reserved pine nuts. Bake for 15 to 20 minutes or until a tester comes out clean. Cool. Makes one dozen muffins.

Prune Nut

2 cups all-purpose flour
2/3 cup granulated sugar
2 teaspoons baking powder
1/2 teaspoon baking soda
1/2 teaspoon salt
1 tablespoon grated orange zest
   (rind or peel)

2/3 cup coarsely chopped pecans
1 cup coarsely chopped cooked
   prunes
2/3 cup orange juice
1 large egg
1/4 cup melted butter

Directions:

Heat oven to 350°. In a large bowl, sift together the flour, sugar, baking powder, baking soda, and salt. Add the orange zest, pecans, and prunes. Mix until the fruits and nuts are coated. In a medium bowl, beat together the orange juice, egg and butter. Pour the orange juice mixture into the flour mixture. Fold until well blended. Do not overmix. Fill greased muffin tins. Bake for 15 to 20 minutes or until a tester inserted into a muffin comes out clean. Makes one dozen muffins.

A fruit-and-nut breakfast treat that tastes even more sensational spread with cream cheese.

Multigrain

1 1/2 cups buttermilk
1/2 cup corn oil
2 eggs
1/4 cup honey
1/4 cup molasses
2 cups sifted all-purpose flour
1/2 cup granulated sugar
1 teaspoon baking soda

1 teaspoon salt
1 1/2 cups bran flakes
1/2 cup rolled oats
1/2 cup golden raisins
1/2 cup dates
1/3 cup walnuts
1/4 cup sunflower seeds

Directions:

   Heat oven to 350°. In a medium bowl, mix together the buttermilk, corn oil, and eggs. Stir in the honey and molasses. In a large bowl, mix together the flour, sugar, baking soda, salt, bran flakes, and oats. Stir in the raisins, dates, walnuts, and sunflower seeds.

   Combine the buttermilk mixture with the dry ingredients and mix until blended. Fill greased muffin tins three-fourths full. Bake for 18 to 20 minutes or until a tester inserted into a muffin comes out clean. Makes two dozen muffins.

   Start your day with these energizing breakfast treats packed with lots of healthy crunch!

Chunky Granola

2 cups granola
1 cup all-purpose flour
1/3 cup firmly packed light-brown
    sugar
2 teaspoons baking powder
1/2 teaspoon ground cinnamon
1/2 teaspoon salt

1/2 cup milk
1/3 cup butter, melted
1 egg, slightly beaten
1 teaspoon vanilla
1/2 cup golden raisins
1/3 cup slivered almonds
1/2 cup flaked coconut

Directions:

    Heat oven to 400°. In a large bowl, stir together the granola, flour, brown sugar, baking powder, cinnamon, and salt. In another bowl, blend together the milk, butter, egg, and vanilla. Make a well in the center of the dry ingredients. Add milk mixture and stir just to combine.. Stir in the raisins, almonds, and coconut. Fill greased muffin tins. Bake 15 to 20 minutes, or until a tester comes out clean. Cool. Makes one dozen muffins.

Breakfast in a Muffin

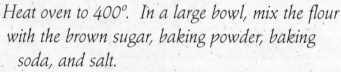

Golden Bran

1 cup all-purpose flour
1/3 cup dark brown sugar, firmly packed
1 1/2 teaspoons baking powder
1 1/2 teaspoons baking soda
1/4 teaspoon salt

1 1/2 cups bran flakes
1 1/3 cups lowfat buttermilk
1 egg
1/3 cup corn oil
1/2 cup golden raisins

Directions:

Heat oven to 400°. In a large bowl, mix the flour with the brown sugar, baking powder, baking soda, and salt.

In another bowl, combine the bran flakes and buttermilk and let stand about 3 minutes. Add the egg, corn oil, and golden raisins. Stir well.

Add the buttermilk mixture to the flour mixture and mix just enough to moisten the flour. Pour the batter into greased muffin tins. Bake for 18 minutes or until the muffins are golden brown. Makes one dozen muffins.

Hominy and Cheddar Cheese

1 (15 ounce) can of hominy grits
1 tablespoon olive oil or butter
2 cups minus 2 tablespoons
  all-purpose flour
1 tablespoon baking powder
2 teaspoons baking soda
1/4 teaspoon salt
4 tablespoons granulated sugar
1 egg
1/4 teaspoon dry mustard
1 cup lowfat milk
1/2 cup melted butter
1 cup shredded cheddar cheese

Directions:

Heat oven to 375°. In a small frying pan, cook the grits in one tablespoon of olive oil or butter over medium heat for 5 minutes. In a large bowl, sift together the flour, baking powder, baking soda, salt, and sugar.

In a medium-sized bowl, lightly beat the egg. Add the dry mustard, milk, and melted butter. Mix together and pour into the flour mixture. Add the grits and cheddar cheese. Stir just until blended. Fill greased muffin tins full. Bake for 18 minutes or until a tester inserted into a muffin comes out clean. Makes one dozen muffins.

Honey Bran

2 cups bran flakes
1 cup all-purpose flour
1 cup cake flour
1/8 teaspoon salt
1 teaspoon baking soda

1/2 cup light brown sugar
3 eggs
1 cup milk
1/2 cup corn oil
1/2 cup honey
1 cup raisins

Directions:

Heat oven to 400°. In a large bowl, combine the bran flakes, the all-purpose and cake flours, salt, baking soda, and brown sugar. Add the eggs, milk, corn oil, and honey. Blend well with a mixer. Stir in the raisins. Fill greased muffin tins. Bake for 20 minutes. Makes 18 muffins.

Honey sweetens the bran in these tasty muffins. . .

Hunter Style

1/2 lb. ground chuck
1/4 cup fresh onion, minced
1/4 cup green pepper
1/2 cup stewed tomatoes
1 tablespoon Worcestershire sauce
1/2 teaspoon pepper
5 dashes Tabasco sauce
2 cups minus 2 tablespoons all-purpose flour

1 tablespoon baking powder
1/2 teaspoon baking soda
1/2 teaspoon salt
1/2 cup milk, plus juice from the tomatoes to equal one cup
4 tablespoons meat drippings or a combination of bacon fat, margarine, or oil to equal 4 tablespoons

Directions:

Heat oven to 375°. Brown the ground chuck in a frying pan. Add the onion and green pepper. Cook until the onion is translucent. Drain and save the drippings. Add the stewed tomatoes, Worcestershire sauce, pepper, and Tabasco™ sauce to the ground chuck. Simmer for 5 minutes.

Meanwhile, in a large bowl, sift together the flour, baking powder, baking soda, and salt. In a large measuring cup, combine 1/2 cup milk and the juice from the tomatoes to equal 1 cup. Add 4 tablespoons meat drippings, (bacon fat, margarine, or oil.) Add the liquid ingredients to the flour mixture and stir until blended. Add the meat and vegetables and mix well. Fill greased muffin tins full. Bake for 18 minutes or until the muffins are lightly browned. Serve warm. Refrigerate leftovers. Makes one dozen muffins.

Slice these muffins horizontally in half and top with a poached egg for a satisfying, hearty breakfast.

Oatmeal Applesauce

1 1/2 cups rolled oats
1 1/4 cups sifted all-purpose flour
1 1/2 teaspoons baking powder
1 teaspoon baking soda
1 teaspoon ground cinnamon
1/2 cup packed light brown sugar
1 cup applesauce
1/2 cup milk
1 teaspoon vanilla extract

3 tablespoons corn oil
1 egg

Topping
1/2 cup rolled oats
2 tablespoons brown sugar
1/4 teaspoon cinnamon
2 tablespoons melted butter

Directions:

Heat oven to 375°. In a large bowl, mix together the oats, flour, baking powder, baking soda, and cinnamon. In a medium bowl, combine the brown sugar, applesauce, milk, vanilla extract, corn oil, and egg. Add to the flour mixture and stir just until the dry ingredients are moistened.

Fill greased muffin tins. Stir together the oats, brown sugar, cinnamon, and melted butter for the topping and sprinkle over the batter. Bake for 20 minutes or until a tester comes out clean. Makes one dozen muffins.

Fruity Oatmeal

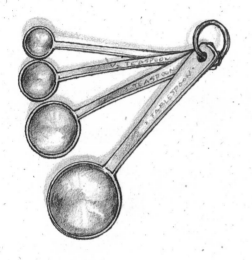

1 1/2 cups rolled oats
3/4 cup whole-wheat flour
1/2 cup sifted all-purpose flour
1/2 cup packed light brown sugar
3 tablespoons oat bran
1 1/2 teaspoons baking powder
1 teaspoon ground cinnamon
3/4 teaspoon baking soda
1/4 teaspoon salt
1/3 cup golden raisins
1/3 cup broken dried banana chips
1/4 cup chopped dates
1/2 cup chopped walnuts
1 cup milk
1/3 cup corn oil
2 eggs, lightly beaten

Directions:
   Heat oven to 400°.
In a large bowl, combine
the oats, the whole-wheat and
all-purpose flours, brown sugar,
oat bran, baking powder, cinnamon,
baking soda, and salt. Mix well. Add raisins, banana chips, dates, and
walnuts. Stir to coat.
   In a small bowl, combine the milk, oil, and eggs. Add the milk mixture to
the flour mixture. Stir just until the dry ingredients are moistened. (Batter will
be lumpy.) Fill greased muffin tins full. Bake for 15 minutes or until a tester
comes out clean. Makes one dozen muffins.

Oatmeal Peach

1 (16 ounce) can of peaches
1 teaspoon baking soda
10 tablespoons butter, softened
1 cup granulated sugar
2 eggs
1/2 teaspoon vanilla extract
1 1/4 cups all-purpose flour
1/4 teaspoon salt
1 1/2 cups rolled oats

Directions:

Heat oven to 350°. Purée the peaches in a blender or food processor. In a small bowl, stir the baking soda into the puréed peaches (this will cause them to foam). Set aside. In a large bowl, cream the butter with the sugar. When the mixture is smooth, add the eggs, one at a time, and then the vanilla extract. In a medium bowl, sift together the flour and salt. Stir in the rolled oats.

Alternately add the flour mixture and the peach purée to the creamed butter and egg mixture. Stir until the ingredients are blended. Fill greased muffin tins. Bake for 20 to 25 minutes or until a tester inserted into a muffin comes out clean. Makes one dozen muffins.

Oatmeal Raisin Cinnamon

1/3 cup shortening
1/2 cup packed light brown sugar
2 eggs
1 cup buttermilk
1 1/4 cups all-purpose flour

1 1/2 teaspoons ground cinnamon
1 teaspoon salt
1 teaspoon baking soda
1 teaspoon baking powder
1 1/2 cups rolled oats
1 cup golden raisins

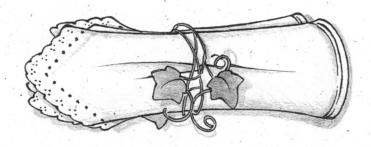

Directions:

Heat oven to 400°. In a large bowl, beat together the shortening and brown sugar. Add eggs and buttermilk and mix until blended. In another bowl, sift together the flour, cinnamon, salt, baking soda, and baking powder. Stir in the oats.

Fold the flour mixture and raisins into the buttermilk mixture with a rubber spatula. Fill greased muffin tins. Bake 18 to 20 minutes or until a tester inserted into a muffin comes out clean. Makes one dozen muffins.

Indulge your family at breakfast with this delicious alternative to that ordinary bowl of cereal.

Orange Oat Bran

1 cup rolled oats
1/2 cup chopped figs
1 1/4 cups orange juice
1 1/2 cups uncooked oat bran
1 cup sifted all-purpose flour
1/2 cup powdered milk
2 teaspoons baking powder
1/2 teaspoon baking soda
1/4 teaspoon salt
1/2 cup packed dark or light brown sugar
1/2 cup corn oil
2 large eggs
1 teaspoon orange zest (rind or peel)

Directions:

Heat oven to 375°. In a large bowl, soak the oats and figs in the orange juice for 15 minutes. In a medium bowl, mix the oat bran, flour, powdered milk, baking powder, baking soda, and salt. Into the soaked oat mixture, add the brown sugar, corn oil, eggs, and orange zest. Stir until well blended.

Add the flour mixture. Stir just until the dry ingredients are moistened. Fill greased muffin tins. Bake 20 to 25 minutes or until the muffins are lightly browned. Makes 14 muffins.

Wheat

2 cups whole-wheat flour
2 teaspoons baking powder
1 teaspoon baking soda
1 teaspoon ground cinnamon
1/4 teaspoon salt
1/4 cup dark brown sugar

2 eggs
1 cup buttermilk
1/4 cup corn oil
2 tablespoons dark molasses
1/2 cup raisins

Directions:

Heat oven to 350°. In a large bowl, mix together the wheat flour, baking powder, baking soda, cinnamon, salt, and brown sugar. In a medium bowl, lightly beat the eggs, buttermilk, corn oil, and molasses. Pour the egg mixture into the flour mixture and stir until the dry ingredients are moistened. Stir in the raisins. Fill greased muffin tins. Bake for 18 to 20 minutes or until a tester inserted into a muffin comes out clean. Cool. Store in an airtight container for 1 day to let the flavors develop. Makes one dozen muffins.

Start the day off right with these wholesome wheat muffins sweetened with raisins.

Yogurt Cinnamon

2 cups minus two tablespoons
  all-purpose flour
1 tablespoon baking powder
1 teaspoon baking soda
2 teaspoons ground cinnamon
1/4 teaspoon ground nutmeg

1/4 cup granulated sugar
1/8 teaspoon salt
1 egg
1/2 cup plain yogurt
4 tablespoons butter, melted
1 1/2 teaspoons vanilla extract

Directions:

Heat oven to 400°. In a medium bowl, sift together the flour, baking powder, baking soda, cinnamon, nutmeg, sugar, and salt. In a large bowl, combine the egg, yogurt, butter, and vanilla extract. Beat together until blended. Add the dry ingredients and stir just until they are moistened. Fill greased muffin tins. Bake 10 to 15 minutes or until the muffins are lightly browned. Serve warm. Makes one dozen muffins.

Sour Cream Streusel

2 cups sifted all-purpose flour
1/2 cup granulated sugar
1 tablespoon baking powder
1 egg
1/2 cup melted butter
8 ounces sour cream
1 teaspoon vanilla extract

Streusel Topping:
1/3 cup granulated sugar
1/4 teaspoon cinnamon
3 tablespoons butter
1/3 cup chopped walnuts

Directions:

Heat oven to 400°. In a large bowl, sift together the flour, sugar, and baking powder. In another bowl, lightly beat the egg. Add the melted butter, sour cream, and vanilla extract. Combine well. Add the sour cream mixture to the flour mixture and mix just until the ingredients are combined. Fill greased muffin tins with batter.

To make the streusel topping, mix the sugar and cinnamon together. Cut in the butter with a pastry blender. Stir in the walnuts.

Sprinkle the streusel topping over the batter. Bake 15 to 20 minutes or until a tester inserted into the center of a muffin comes out clean. Makes one dozen muffins.

This recipe is so easy to make and so good!

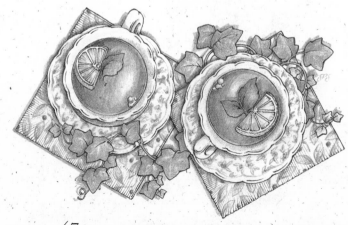

Ham and Cheese

1 egg
2 tablespoons granulated sugar
1 cup sour cream
1 tablespoon corn oil
1 teaspoon prepared mustard
1 1/3 cups sifted all-purpose flour

1 teaspoon baking powder
1/2 teaspoon baking soda
1/2 teaspoon salt
1 cup diced cooked ham
1/2 cup shredded Swiss cheese

Directions:

Heat oven to 400°. In a large bowl, lightly beat the egg. Add the sugar, sour cream, corn oil, and mustard. Mix well. Add the flour, baking powder, baking soda, and salt. Stir just until the dry ingredients are moistened. Gently stir in the ham and cheese. Fill greased muffin tins. Bake for 20 to 25 minutes or until the muffins are brown. Makes one dozen muffins.

Everyone will enjoy this ham and cheese combination served in a surprisingly new way in a breakfast muffin.

For Chocolate Lovers

Chocolate Caramel

2 cups all-purpose flour
1 tablespoon baking powder
1/2 teaspoon salt
1/3 cup granulated sugar
1 cup milk

1 egg
1/3 cup corn oil
20 caramels
1 tablespoon water
2 15-ounce milk chocolate bars

Directions:

Heat oven to 400°. In a large bowl, sift together the flour, baking powder, salt, and sugar. In another bowl, mix together the milk, egg, and corn oil. Add the milk mixture to the flour mixture and stir just until the dry ingredients are moistened. Chop the chocolate bars into small pieces and stir into the batter.

Put the caramels into a bowl with one tablespoon of water and melt them in a microwave oven by cooking them on a high setting for 2 minutes. Note: Be careful not to burn the caramels.

Spoon 1 heaping tablespoon of batter into each greased muffin tin. Add a layer of 1 teaspoon of melted caramel. Top with another tablespoon of batter. Bake for 20 minutes or until the muffins are brown. Makes one dozen muffins.

A great way to use up leftover Halloween candy!

Chocolate Orange

1 cup granulated sugar
1/2 cup softened butter
2 large eggs
Zest from 2 large oranges (rind or peel)
6-ounces orange yogurt
1/2 cup freshly squeezed orange juice

1/2 teaspoon baking soda
1 teaspoon baking powder
2 cups sifted all-purpose flour
3 ounces bittersweet chocolate

Directions:

Heat oven to 375°. In a large bowl, cream the sugar and butter with a mixer until fluffy. Beat in the eggs, one at a time. Add the orange zest, orange yogurt, orange juice, baking powder, and baking soda. Mix well. Chop the chocolate into small pieces. Fold the flour and chocolate into the orange mixture. Pour the batter into greased muffin tins. Bake 20 minutes or until the muffins are golden brown. Makes one dozen muffins.

Fudge

5 ounces semisweet chocolate, coarsely chopped

3 ounces unsweetened chocolate, coarsely chopped

1/3 cup butter

3/4 cup sour cream

2/3 cup firmly packed light brown sugar

1/4 cup light corn syrup

1 egg

1 1/4 teaspoons vanilla extract

1 1/2 cups all-purpose flour

1 teaspoon baking soda

1/4 teaspoon salt

1 cup semisweet chocolate chips

Directions:

Heat oven to 400°. Melt the first three ingredients in a double boiler. Cool slightly; then pour into a medium bowl. Using a whisk, stir in the sour cream, brown sugar, corn syrup, egg, and vanilla extract into the melted chocolate. In a large bowl, mix together the flour, baking soda, salt, and chocolate chips.

Make a well in the center of the dry ingredients. Add the chocolate mixture to the well and stir until the ingredients are blended. Spoon the batter into greased or foil-lined muffin tins. Bake the muffins 20 minutes or until a tester inserted into the center comes out clean. Serve warm. Makes about 16 muffins.

Mint Chocolate Chip

1 1/4 cups all-purpose flour
1 tablespoon baking powder
1/4 teaspoon salt
1/4 cup powdered cocoa
3/4 cup granulated sugar

1/4 teaspoon cinnamon
1 egg
1/4 cup corn oil
2/3 cup milk
1 teaspoon mint extract
1 cup miniature chocolate chips

Directions:

Heat oven to 375°. In a large bowl, sift together the flour, baking powder, and salt. Stir in the cocoa, sugar, and cinnamon. In a medium bowl, lightly beat the egg. Stir in the corn oil, milk, and mint extract.

Add the egg mixture to the flour mixture and stir in the chocolate chips. Stir just until the dry ingredients are moistened. Fill greased muffin tins. Bake for 18 minutes or until a tester comes out clean. Makes one dozen muffins.

Tunnelfudge

1/2 cup butter
1/3 cup water
5 squares semisweet chocolate
5 tablespoons cocoa
2/3 cup granulated sugar
2 cups all-purpose flour
1 tablespoon baking powder
1/4 teaspoon salt
1 egg
1/2 cup milk
1/2 cup sour cream
2 teaspoons vanilla extract
12 Hershey Kisses™ candies

Directions:

Heat oven to 375°. In a small saucepan, melt the butter over low heat. Add the water and semisweet chocolate squares and stir until the chocolate is melted. Cool.

In a large bowl, sift together the flour, baking powder, and salt. In another bowl, combine the egg, milk, sour cream, and vanilla extract and blend on low speed with an electric mixer. Make a well in the center of the dry ingredients, and pour in the egg mixture and the cooled chocolate mixture. Blend at medium speed.

Fill greased muffin tins. Take one Hershey Kisses candy and push it down into the center of each cup of batter. Bake for 20 minutes or until a tester comes out clean. (Insert the tester off center to avoid the candy.) Cool. Makes one dozen muffins.

Zucchini Chocolate

1 1/2 cups shredded zucchini
1/2 teaspoon salt
2 cups all-purpose flour
1 teaspoon baking soda
1 tablespoon baking powder
2 teaspoons cinnamon
1/2 teaspoon ground cloves
1/4 cup cocoa

1 cup coarsely chopped walnuts
1 cup semisweet chocolate chips
1/3 cup corn oil
2 teaspoon vanilla extract
3 eggs, beaten
1 cup granulated sugar
1/2 cup buttermilk

Directions:

Heat oven to 375°. Shred the zucchini, place it in a small bowl, and sprinkle it with 1/2 teaspoon salt. Set aside. In a large bowl, sift together the flour, baking soda, baking powder, cinnamon, and cloves. Stir in the cocoa.

Toast the walnuts in the oven for 4 minutes. Stir the walnuts and chocolate chips into the flour mixture. In a medium bowl, mix together the corn oil, vanilla extract, eggs, sugar, and buttermilk. Add the buttermilk mixture to the flour mixture and mix well. Stir in the zucchini. Fill greased muffin tins. Bake for 20 minutes or until a tester inserted into the center of a muffin comes out clean. Makes 18 muffins.

No one will ever know that there's a vegetable in these muffins!

Banana Chocolate

4 tablespoons butter
6 tablespoons cocoa
4 tablespoons hot water
1 1/4 cups all-purpose flour
1/2 cup granulated sugar
1 tablespoon baking powder
1 teaspoon ground cinnamon

1/4 teaspoon salt
2/3 cup milk
1 large egg
1 teaspoon vanilla extract
2 mashed bananas
1/2 cup semisweet chocolate
  chips
Confectioners' sugar

Directions:

Heat oven to 375°. Melt the butter in a microwave oven or in a saucepan. Combine the cocoa and the hot water with the melted butter. Let it cool slightly. In a large bowl, sift together the flour, sugar, baking powder, cinnamon, and salt. Using a wire whisk or fork, beat the milk, egg and vanilla extract in a small bowl, blending well.

Cut up the bananas, mash slightly, and add them to the milk mixture with the cooled chocolate mixture. Pour the milk mixture into the dry ingredients, stirring just until blended. Stir in the chocolate chips. Pour the batter into greased muffin tins. Bake 22 to 25 minutes or until the tops of the muffins spring back when pressed lightly with a finger. Sprinkle the tops of the muffins with confectioners' sugar. Serve warm or at room temperature. Makes one dozen muffins.

Peanut Butter Chocolate

1 3/4 cups all-purpose flour
1 tablespoon baking powder
1/4 teaspoon salt
3 tablespoons cocoa
1/2 cup granulated sugar
6 tablespoons melted butter

3/4 cup creamy peanut butter
2/3 cup milk
1 large egg
1 teaspoon vanilla extract
1/2 cup semisweet chocolate chips

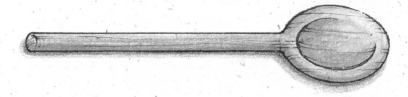

Directions:
   Heat oven to 375°. In a large bowl, sift together the flour, baking powder, and salt. Stir in the cocoa and sugar. In a medium bowl, beat the peanut butter, melted butter, milk, egg, and vanilla extract until the mixture is smooth. Pour the peanut butter mixture and the chocolate chips into the flour mixture. Stir until blended. The batter will be stiff. Fill greased muffin tins full. Bake for 20 minutes or until a tester inserted in a muffin comes out clean. Makes one dozen muffins.

Mocha Chocolate Chip

1/4 cup hot water
1 tablespoon instant coffee granules
1/2 cup corn oil
1/2 cup buttermilk
1 teaspoon vanilla
1/2 cup firmly packed
   light-brown sugar
2 eggs, lightly beaten
1 3/4 cups all-purpose
   flour

1 teaspoon baking powder
1 teaspoon baking soda
1 teaspoon salt
1/2 cup sugar
2 tablespoons cocoa powder
1 6 oz. package semisweet
   chocolate chips
1 cup coarsely chopped
   pecans

Directions:

Heat oven to 375°. Place the hot water into a medium-sized bowl. Stir in the instant coffee granules and dissolve. Add the corn oil, buttermilk, vanilla, and brown sugar. Combine well. Whisk in the eggs. In a large bowl, sift together the flour, baking powder, baking soda, and salt. Stir in the sugar and cocoa powder. Add the buttermilk mixture and stir just until combined. Mix in the chocolate chips and pecans. Fill greased muffin tins. Bake 20 to 22 minutes, or until a tester comes out clean. Cool. Makes 16 muffins.

Variations on a Cake

Apple Cheesecake

1/3 cup ricotta cheese

3 ounces cream cheese

1/4 cup granulated sugar

2 teaspoons vanilla extract

1 tablespoon sweetened condensed milk

1/8 teaspoon nutmeg

2 cups minus 2 tablespoons all-purpose flour

1 tablespoon baking powder

1/4 teaspoon salt

5 tablespoons melted butter

1/3 cup sweetened condensed milk

2/3 cup apple juice

1 egg

1 cup diced Granny Smith apple

Directions:

Heat oven to 375°. In a medium bowl, beat together the ricotta cheese, cream cheese, and sugar. (Note: Do not soften the cream cheese.) Add the vanilla extract, 1 tablespoon sweetened condensed milk, and nutmeg. In a large bowl, sift together the flour, baking powder, and salt.

In a small bowl, mix together the melted butter, 1/3 cup sweetened condensed milk, apple juice, and the egg. Pour this mixture into the dry ingredients and stir just until moistened. Gently stir in the diced apple. Drop one tablespoon of batter into each greased muffin tin and smooth the batter to distribute it evenly. Place 1 tablespoon of the ricotta cheese mixture on the batter and then top that with one more tablespoon of batter. Bake for 15 minutes until the muffins are lightly browned. Makes one dozen muffins.

Cherry Cheesecake

2 cups minus 2 tablespoons
   all-purpose flour
1/4 teaspoon salt
2 tablespoons granulated sugar
1 tablespoon baking powder

1 egg
4 tablespoons melted butter
6 ounces cream cheese,
   softened
1/2 cup sweetened condensed
   milk
1 (16 ounce) can dark, sweet
   cherries, drained
1/2 cup cherry juice (saved
   from the can of dark
   cherries)

Directions:

Heat oven to 375°. In a large bowl, sift together the flour, salt, sugar, and baking powder. In another bowl, beat the egg with a hand mixer on low speed. Then blend in the melted butter, cream cheese, and sweetened condensed milk. Measure the cherry juice and add enough water to equal 1 cup. Blend this into the cream cheese mixture. Stir in the cherries by hand.

Pour the cream cheese mixture into the flour mixture and mix by hand just until the dry ingredients are moistened. Fill greased muffin tins. Bake 20 minutes or until the muffins are brown. Makes one dozen muffins.

Enjoy this cherry jubilee with your favorite tea or with a cup of freshly brewed coffee.

Lemon Cheesecake

1/3 cup ricotta cheese
3 ounces cream cheese
1/2 cup granulated sugar
1 teaspoon vanilla extract
1/4 teaspoon lemon extract
2 cups minus 2 tablespoons
   all-purpose flour
1 tablespoon baking powder

1/4 teaspoon salt
Zest of two lemons (rind or peel)
2/3 cup fresh lemon juice
1 egg
5 tablespoons melted butter
1/3 cup sweetened condensed
   milk

Directions:

Heat oven to 375°. In a medium bowl, beat together the ricotta cheese, cream cheese, and 1/4 cup sugar. (Note: Do not soften the cream cheese) Add the vanilla and lemon extracts. In a large bowl, sift together the flour, baking powder, and salt. Use a lemon zestor or grater to get the zest of 2 lemons. Then process or squeeze approximately 4 lemons to make 2/3 cup lemon juice. Combine the lemon juice, zest, and the remainder of the sugar in a small bowl. Add a lightly beaten egg, the melted butter, and 1/3 cup sweetened condensed milk.

Pour this mixture into the flour mixture and stir until the dry ingredients are moistened. Drop one tablespoon of batter into each greased muffin tin. Smooth the batter and then top with 1 tablespoon of the ricotta cheese mixture followed by 1 more table-spoon of batter. Bake for 15 minutes or until the muffins are lightly browned. Makes one dozen muffins.

Lemon Shortbread

2 cups all-purpose flour
2 teaspoons baking powder
2 teaspoons baking soda
1/2 teaspoon salt
2 tablespoons granulated sugar
2 eggs

1/4 cup corn oil
1 cup lemon yogurt
1 tablespoon lemon juice
1 tablespoon lemon zest
   (rind or peel)
1 teaspoon lemon extract

Directions:

Heat oven to 400°. In a large bowl, sift together the flour, baking powder, baking soda, salt, and sugar. In a medium bowl, lightly beat the eggs. Add the corn oil, yogurt, lemon juice, lemon zest, and lemon extract. Mix well. Stir the egg mixture into the flour mixture until the ingredients are blended.

Fill greased muffin tins. Bake for 15 to 20 minutes or until the muffins are brown. Makes one dozen muffins. Serve warm.

Pineapple Upside-Up

2 1/4 cups all-purpose flour
1 tablespoon baking powder
1/2 teaspoon salt
1/2 cup light brown sugar
1/2 cup coconut
1 egg
1/4 cup corn oil
1/4 cup melted butter
1/3 cup milk
1 teaspoon vanilla extract
1 cup crushed pineapple,
  undrained

Topping
2 tablespoons butter
7 tablespoons light brown sugar
7 tablespoons chopped walnuts

Directions:

Heat oven to 400°. In a large bowl, sift together the flour, baking powder, and salt. Stir in the brown sugar and coconut. In another bowl, mix the egg, corn oil, butter, milk, vanilla extract, and pineapple. Stir the pineapple mixture into the dry ingredients just until moistened.

Fill greased muffin tins. Make the topping by cutting the butter into the brown sugar and stirring in the walnuts. Sprinkle the topping over the batter. Bake for 20 minutes or until the muffins are a golden brown. Makes one dozen muffins.

These superb little cakes will win raves all around!

Poppy Seed Cheese

3/4 cup ricotta cheese
1 egg white, slightly beaten
4 teaspoons granulated sugar
1 1/4 cups rolled oats
1 1/4 cups sifted all-purpose flour
1/3 cup granulated sugar
3 tablespoons poppy seeds
1 tablespoon baking powder
1/4 teaspoon salt
1 cup milk
3 tablespoons corn oil
2 eggs

Directions:

Heat oven to 375°. In a small bowl, combine the ricotta cheese, egg white, and 4 teaspoons sugar. Set aside. In a large bowl, mix together the oats, flour, 1/3 cup sugar, poppy seeds, baking powder, and salt. In another bowl, combine the milk, oil, and eggs.

Pour the milk mixture into the oat mixture and mix just until the dry ingredients are moistened. Spoon 1 tablespoon of batter into each greased muffin tin. Add 1 tablespoon of the ricotta cheese mixture. Top with 1 more tablespoon of batter. Bake for 22 to 25 minutes or until the muffins are lightly browned. Makes one dozen muffins.

The ricotta cheese filling is a taste surprise in these marvelous muffins!

Almond

1/2 cup softened butter
1/2 cup granulated sugar
2 large eggs
1 teaspoon almond extract

1 cup plain yogurt
8 ounces almond filling
2 cups all-purpose flour
1 teaspoon baking powder

1/2 teaspoon baking soda

Directions:

Heat oven to 350°. In a large bowl, cream the butter with a mixer. Beat in the sugar until the mixture is fluffy. Add the eggs, one at a time, then the almond extract, yogurt, and almond filling. Mix until blended.

In a medium bowl, sift together the flour, baking powder, and baking soda. Fold the flour mixture into the egg mixture with a spatula.

Fill greased muffin tins. Bake the muffins 25 to 30 minutes until they are lightly browned. Makes one dozen muffins.

Black Forest

1 (6 oz.) package semisweet
  chocolate chips
1/4 cup butter
1/2 cup buttermilk
1/2 cup sugar
1 egg, lightly beaten
2 tablespoons brandy

1 1/2 teaspoons vanilla
1 (16.5 oz.) can pitted, dark
  sweet cherries, chopped and
  drained
1 3/4 cups all-purpose flour
1 teaspoon baking soda
1/2 teaspoon salt

Directions:

Heat oven to 400°. In a small saucepan, melt chocolate with butter over
low heat. Cool. In a small bowl, stir chocolate mixture with buttermilk,
sugar, egg, brandy, and vanilla until blended.
Stir in cherries. In a large bowl, stir
together flour, baking soda, and salt.
Make a well in the center
of the dry ingredients. Add
the chocolate mixture and stir
just to combine. Fill greased
muffin tins. Bake 20 to 25
minutes, or until a tester
comes out clean. Cool.
Makes one dozen muffins.

Lemon Poppy Seed

2 cups sifted all-purpose flour
1/4 cup poppy seeds
1/2 teaspoon salt
1/4 teaspoon baking soda
1 cup sugar
1/3 cup corn oil

1/2 cup milk
1/4 cup freshly squeezed lemon
   juice
2 eggs, lightly beaten
2 teaspoons vanilla

Directions:

   Heat oven to 350°. In a large bowl, stir together the flour, poppy seeds, salt, baking soda, and sugar. In a small bowl, blend together the milk, lemon juice, eggs, and vanilla. Pour the liquid mixture into the dry ingredients and mix well. Fill greased muffin tins. Bake 20 minutes, or until a tester comes out clean. Cool. Makes one dozen muffins.

Four Chip

2 cups all-purpose flour
1/2 cup firmly packed light-
   brown sugar
2 teaspoons baking powder
1/2 teaspoon salt
2/3 cup milk
1/2 cup butter, melted
2 eggs, lightly beaten
1 teaspoon vanilla
1/2 cup semisweet chocolate chips
1/2 cup white chocolate morsels
1/2 cup butterscotch chips
1/2 cup peanut butter chips
1/2 cup chopped walnuts

Directions:

Heat oven to 350°. In a large bowl, stir together the flour, brown sugar, baking powder, and salt. In another bowl, blend together the milk, butter, eggs, and vanilla. Make a well in the center of the dry ingredients. Add the milk mixture and stir just to combine. Stir in the chips and nuts. Fill greased muffin tins. Bake 15 to 20 minutes, or until a tester comes out clean. Cool. Makes one dozen muffins.

Lemon Coconut

1 3/4 cups sifted all-purpose flour
3/4 cup granulated sugar
1/2 cup coconut
1 tablespoon grated lemon zest
   (rind or peel)
1 teaspoon baking powder
3/4 teaspoon baking soda
1/4 teaspoon salt
8 ounces lemon yogurt

6 tablespoons melted butter
1 egg
1 tablespoon fresh lemon juice

Glaze
1/3 cup fresh lemon juice
1/4 cup granulated sugar
1/4 cup toasted coconut

Directions:

Heat oven to 400°. In a large bowl, mix together the flour, sugar, coconut, lemon zest, baking powder, baking soda, and salt. Make a well in the center of the ingredients. In another bowl, whisk together the yogurt, melted butter, egg, and lemon juice. Pour the yogurt mixture into the well in the dry ingredients. Stir just until blended. The batter will be lumpy.

Spoon the batter into greased muffin tins. Bake for 20 minutes or until the muffins are golden brown. While the muffins are baking, make the glaze by cooking the lemon juice, sugar, and toasted coconut in a small non-aluminum saucepan over low heat until the sugar dissolves.

Cool the muffins in the pan for 5 minutes, then transfer them to a rack set over a baking sheet. Pierce 6 to 8 holes in the top of each muffin with a toothpick. Drizzle the hot glaze over the muffins, coating the tops well. Serve at room temperature.
Makes one dozen muffins.

For The Little Ones

Bacon Brown Sugar

10 slices bacon
1 cup buttermilk
1 cup maple syrup
2 eggs
3/4 cup whole-wheat flour
3/4 cup all-purpose flour

1/2 cup firmly packed dark brown
   sugar
3/4 teaspoon salt
2 teaspoons baking powder
1 teaspoon baking soda
1 cup rolled oats

Directions:

Heat oven to 350°. Fry the bacon until it is crisp. Drain and crumble into small pieces. In a large bowl, whisk together the buttermilk, maple syrup, and eggs. Add the whole-wheat and all-purpose flours, brown sugar, salt, baking powder, baking soda, and oats. Mix well. Stir in the bacon. Fill greased muffin tins three fourths full. Bake about 20 minutes or until a tester inserted into the center comes out clean. Makes 18 muffins.

These breakfast of pancakes and bacon.

muffins combine the flavors Delicious!

Gingerbread

1/2 cup shortening
3/4 cup granulated sugar
2 beaten eggs
1/4 cup milk
1/2 cup light molasses
2 cup sifted all-purpose flour
1 teaspoon baking soda
1 teaspoon baking powder
1 teaspoon ground cinnamon
1 teaspoon ground ginger
1/4 teaspoon salt

Directions:

Heat oven to 400°. In a large bowl, cream the shortening. Beat in the sugar until fluffy. Add the eggs, milk, and molasses. Mix well. In another bowl, sift together the flour, baking soda, baking powder, cinnamon, ginger, and salt. Stir into the molasses mixture. Blend well. Fill greased muffin tins. Bake 15 minutes or until a tester inserted into the muffins comes out clean. Makes one dozen muffins.

These fragrant treats can be topped with vanilla frosting and served for dessert.

Jam

1 3/4 cups all-purpose flour
2 1/2 teaspoons baking powder
1/2 teaspoon salt
3/4 cup milk
1 egg
1/3 cup corn oil
1/2 cup granulated sugar
1/4 cup jam (any flavor that you prefer)

Directions:

Heat oven to 400°. In a large bowl, sift together the flour, baking powder, and salt. In a medium bowl, mix together the milk, egg, corn oil, and sugar. Stir the milk mixture into the flour mixture until the dry ingredients are moistened. Let sit for 1 minute.

Spoon 2 tablespoons of the batter into greased muffin tins. Spread one teaspoon of jam over the batter. Top with 2 tablespoons of batter. Bake for 20 minutes or until the muffins are brown. Makes one dozen muffins.

Kids will love to find this muffin surprise in their lunch bags!

Peanut Butter and Jelly

2 cups all-purpose flour
1 tablespoon baking powder
3 tablespoons granulated sugar
3/4 cup creamy peanut butter
1 egg
1 cup milk
1/3 cup strawberry jam or
    grape jelly

Directions:

Heat oven to 350°. In a large bowl, sift together the flour, baking powder, and sugar. In a medium bowl, beat together the peanut butter and egg. Gradually add milk. Pour the peanut butter mixture into the flour mixture and stir just until the dry ingredients are moistened. The batter will be very stiff.

Spoon 1 tablespoon of batter into greased muffin tins. Smooth it with your fingers. Add a heaping teaspoon of jelly and top with one more tablespoon of batter. Bake for 20 minutes or until the muffins are lightly browned. Makes one dozen muffins.

Peanut Butter Bacon

1 3/4 cups all-purpose flour
1/2 cup granulated sugar
1 tablespoon baking powder
1/2 teaspoon salt
3/4 cup milk
1/2 cup creamy peanut butter
1/3 cup corn oil
1 egg
12 slices crisply fried bacon

Directions:

Heat oven to 400°. In a large bowl, sift together the flour, sugar, baking powder, and salt. In a medium bowl, beat together the milk, peanut butter, corn oil, and egg until smooth. Crumble the bacon into the flour mixture. Add the peanut butter mixture and stir until the ingredients are blended. Fill greased muffin tins. Bake 16 to 18 minutes or until a tester inserted in a muffin comes out clean. Makes one dozen muffins.

Banana Peanut Butter

2 cups sifted all-purpose flour
1/2 cup rolled oats
1 tablespoon baking powder
2 small, very ripe mashed bananas
1 cup milk
1 egg, beaten
1/3 cup chunky peanut butter
4 tablespoons corn oil
1 teaspoon vanilla extract
1/2 cup honey

Topping
1/4 cup rolled oats
1/4 cup all-purpose flour
2 tablespoons firmly packed brown
  sugar
Dash cinnamon
2 tablespoons melted butter

Directions:

Heat oven to 375°. In a large bowl, combine the flour, oats, and baking powder. In a small bowl, mash the bananas, then blend them with the milk and egg. Combine the peanut butter, corn oil, vanilla extract, and honey in a medium bowl. Stir in the banana mixture. Pour the peanut butter mixture into the flour mixture, mixing just until the dry ingredients are moistened. Fill greased muffin tins.

To make the topping, combine the oats, flour, brown sugar, cinnamon, and melted butter in a small bowl. Sprinkle the mixture evenly over the batter.

Bake 20 minutes or until the muffins are golden brown. Makes a baker's dozen. Serve warm.

Apple Caramel

2 cups all-purpose flour
1 tablespoon baking powder
3/4 teaspoon cinnamon
1/2 teaspoon nutmeg
3/4 teaspoon salt
1/4 cup granulated sugar
2 eggs, well beaten
1/2 cup milk
3 tablespoons corn oil
1 cup peeled and diced apples

Topping
1/4 cup butter
1/2 cup brown sugar
2 tablespoons milk

1 1/2 cups confectioners' sugar
1 teaspoon vanilla extract
1/4 cup chopped nuts (optional)

Directions:

Heat oven to 400°. Sift the dry ingredients together into a large bowl. Add the eggs, milk, and corn oil. Stir just enough to mix the ingredients. Carefully fold in the diced apples. Fill greased muffin tins.

To make the topping, melt the butter and brown sugar in a saucepan. Stir in the milk and confectioners' sugar until the mixture is smooth. Add the vanilla extract and nuts. Spoon over the top of the muffins. Bake for 25 minutes. Makes one dozen muffins.

Adult Accoutrements

Tipsy Apple

1 cup raisins
1/4 cup brandy
2 cups diced apples (peeled or
  unpeeled)
1 cup granulated sugar
2 eggs, lightly beaten
2 cups applesauce

1/2 cup corn oil
2 teaspoons vanilla extract
2 cups sifted all-purpose flour
1/2 cup toasted rolled oats
2 teaspoons baking soda
2 teaspoons cinnamon
1 teaspoon salt

Directions:

    Heat oven to 350°. Put the raisins into a small bowl and pour in the brandy. Let the raisins soak for 15 minutes. Dice the apples and mix them with the sugar in a large bowl. Set this mixture aside. In a medium sized bowl, lightly beat the eggs and combine them with the applesauce, oil, and vanilla extract. Blend well. Drain the brandy from the raisins and add it to the egg mixture. Set aside the raisins.

    In another medium bowl, combine the flour, oats, baking soda, cinnamon, and salt. Stir with a fork until blended. Pour the egg mixture into the apples and sugar. Mix thoroughly. Next, stir in the flour mixture and the raisins, just until blended. Spoon the batter into greased muffin tins. Bake for 25 minutes, or until a tester inserted into the muffins comes out clean. Serve warm. Makes 18 muffins.

Caraway Cheese

2 cups all-purpose flour
3 teaspoon baking powder
1 teaspoon salt
3/4 teaspoon black pepper
2 tablespoons caraway seeds

1 cup milk
2 eggs
2 tablespoons safflower oil
1 cup shredded Swiss cheese

Directions:

Heat oven to 400°. In a large bowl, sift together the flour, baking powder, salt, and pepper. Stir in the caraway seeds. In another bowl, beat together the milk, eggs, and oil. Pour the egg mixture into the flour mixture and mix just until the dry ingredients are moistened. Fold in the Swiss cheese. Fill greased muffin tins. Bake for 15 minutes or until the muffins are golden brown. Makes one dozen muffins.

Cheddar Cheese and Mustard

2 cups minus 2 tablespoons sifted all
  purpose flour
1 tablespoon baking powder
1/2 teaspoon salt
1/8 teaspoon freshly ground pepper

1 1/2 cups grated sharp cheddar
  cheese
1 large egg
2 tablespoons Dijon mustard
1 cup sour cream
1/4 cup butter, melted
1/4 cup milk

Directions:

  Heat oven to 350°. Thoroughly mix the flour, baking powder, salt, and pepper in a large bowl. Add the cheddar cheese. Blend the flour mixture and the cheese with your fingers to distribute the cheese evenly.

  In a small bowl, beat together the egg and the mustard. Add the sour cream, melted butter, and milk. Mix well. Fold the sour cream mixture gently into the flour mixture just until the dry ingredients are moistened. Fill greased muffin tins. Bake 22 minutes. Cool slightly. Serve warm. Makes one dozen.

Garlic Corn

12 cloves fresh garlic
1 1/4 cups sifted all-purpose flour
3/4 cup cornmeal
1/2 rounded teaspoon salt
1 tablespoon baking powder
1 teaspoon granulated sugar
1 egg
1/2 cup milk
1/4 cup corn oil
2 tablespoons softened butter

Directions:

Heat oven to 400°. Separate 12 cloves of garlic from the head; leave the skin on. Microwave the garlic in 1/2 cup water in a tightly covered bowl for 1 1/2 minutes on medium power. Drain the water into a cup and save it. Combine the flour, cornmeal, salt, baking powder, and sugar in a large bowl. In a small bowl, lightly beat the egg; add the milk and oil. Mix well. Pour the egg mixture into the dry ingredients. Stir until blended.

Fill greased muffin tins. Put one clove of garlic, with its skin still on, in the top center of the batter in each muffin cup. Bake the muffins for 20 minutes or until lightly browned. Let them stand for 5 minutes after removing them from the oven.

Remove the garlic cloves from the muffins. Squeeze the pulp from the garlic cloves into a shallow bowl. Mash the garlic and combine with 1 to 2 tablespoons of softened butter. Spread the garlic butter on the warm muffins. Makes one dozen muffins.

Orange Rum

2 large navel oranges
1/4 cup dark rum
2 eggs
1/4 cup orange juice
1/2 cup granulated sugar

1/2 cup melted butter
2 cups all-purpose flour
2 teaspoons baking powder
1/2 cup sliced almonds
1/2 teaspoon salt
3 teaspoons granulated sugar

Directions:

Heat oven to 400°. Peel the oranges, trim off the pith and the white membrane, and save just the orange flesh. Chop the oranges and put the pieces into a small bowl. Add the dark rum and set aside. In a large bowl, whisk the eggs and orange juice. Add the sugar and butter. Stir well.

Sift together the flour, baking powder, and salt in a small bowl. Add the flour mixture to the egg mixture. Stir until the ingredients are blended. Gently stir in the oranges and rum. Fill greased muffin tins. Sprinkle the batter with the almonds and the granulated sugar. Bake for 15 minutes or until a tester inserted into a muffin comes out clean. Serve warm. Makes one dozen muffins.

Enjoy a taste of the Caribbean with these muffins.

Rum Raisin

1 cup golden raisins
1/2 cup dark rum
1 1/4 cups all-purpose flour
1 tablespoon baking powder
1/2 teaspoon salt
1/2 teaspoon cinnamon

1 egg
1/3 cup melted butter
1 tablespoon light brown sugar
1/3 cup milk
1/2 cup sour cream
3/4 cup cooked rice

Directions:

Heat oven to 375°. In a small bowl, soak the raisins in rum for 10 minutes. In a large bowl, sift together the flour, baking powder, salt, and cinnamon. In a medium bowl, lightly beat the egg. Stir in the melted butter and brown sugar. Add the milk and sour cream and mix well.

Drain the rum from the raisins, reserving 2 tablespoons of rum. Add the rum to the milk mixture. Fold the milk mixture into the flour mixture. Fold in the rice and raisins. Fill greased muffin tins. Bake for 18 to 20 minutes or until the muffins are golden brown. Serve warm. Makes one dozen muffins.

Custard

1 (3-ounce) package vanilla
   pudding and pie filling (cook and
   serve)
1 1/2 cups milk
3/4 cup butter, at room temperature
2/3 cup granulated sugar

2 eggs
1 cup all-purpose flour
1 cup cake flour
3/4 teaspoon salt
1 teaspoon baking soda
1 teaspoon baking powder

Directions:

   Heat oven to 375°. Prepare the vanilla pudding according to the directions on the package, but only use 1 1/2 cups milk. Cool the pudding in the freezer for 10 minutes.

   In a large bowl, beat the butter until it is creamy. Add the sugar and eggs and blend well. In another bowl, sift the two kinds of flour, salt, baking soda, and baking powder. Add the flour mixture to the butter mixture and blend well.

   Remove the pudding from the freezer. Grease muffin tins or use foil liners. Drop one tablespoon of batter into each cup. Layer with one teaspoon of pudding. Top the pudding with one more tablespoon of batter. Bake for 15 minutes or until the muffin tops are lightly browned. Cool completely in the pan. Makes one dozen muffins.

Wine and Cheese

2 cups minus 2 tablespoons
   all-purpose flour
1 tablespoon baking powder
1/4 teaspoon salt
1/2 teaspoon oregano
3 tablespoons grated Parmesan
   cheese

1 cup shredded Swiss cheese
2 eggs
1/2 cup milk
1/2 cup white wine
1/4 teaspoon white wine
   Worcestershire sauce

Directions:

   Heat oven to 375°. In a large bowl, sift together the flour, baking
powder, and salt. Stir in the oregano, and Parmesan and Swiss cheeses.
In another bowl, lightly beat the egg and to it add the milk, white wine,
and Worcestershire sauce and stir. Add the egg mixture to the flour mixture and stir just until the dry ingredients are moistened. Fill greased
muffin tins. Bake for 18 minutes or until the muffins are golden brown.
Serve warm. Makes one dozen muffins.

   Bake these flavorful muffins in mini-muffin tins and serve as an
appetizer at your next party.

Double Date

8 tablespoons vegetable shortening
1/2 cup light brown sugar
1 egg
1/2 cup milk
1 teaspoon vanilla extract
1 cup coarsely chopped dates

1 1/2 cups all-purpose flour
1/2 teaspoon salt
2 teaspoons baking powder

Date butter
1/3 cup melted butter
1/2 cup chopped dates

Directions:

Heat oven to 375°. In a large bowl, beat together the shortening and brown sugar until smooth. Add the egg, milk, and vanilla extract. Beat well. Stir in the chopped dates. In a medium bowl, sift together the flour, salt, and baking powder. Add to the date mixture and stir only until no flour streaks show--do not overmix. Spoon the batter into muffin tins, filling them two thirds full.

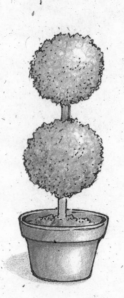

Make a well in the center of the batter in each muffin cup and fill with 1 tablespoon of date butter, which is made by blending 1/3 cup butter with 1/2 cup dates. Bake about 20 minutes or until a tester inserted into the muffins comes out clean. Makes one dozen muffins.

Rice Pudding

1/2 cup raisins
1 1/4 cup all-purpose flour
1/2 teaspoon salt
1 tablespoon baking powder
1/2 cup granulated sugar
3/4 teaspoon cinnamon
1/8 teaspoon nutmeg

1/8 teaspoon nutmeg
1 egg
3/4 cup milk
1/4 cup corn oil
1 teaspoon vanilla extract
3/4 cup cooked rice

Directions:

Heat oven to 375°. In a small bowl, soak the raisins in enough water to cover them. In a large bowl, sift together the flour, salt, baking powder, sugar, cinnamon, and nutmeg. In another bowl, lightly beat the egg. Add the milk, corn oil, and vanilla extract and stir.

Drain the water from the raisins. Fold the raisins and rice into the flour mixture. Add the egg mixture to the flour mixture and stir just until the dry ingredients are moistened. Fill greased muffin tins. Bake for 18 to 20 minutes or until the muffins are golden brown. Makes one dozen muffins. Serve warm.

This recipe could substitute for rice pudding!

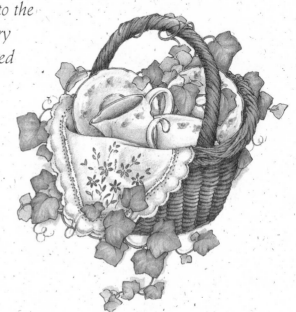

Oatmeal Sunflower

2 cups all-purpose flour
1 cup rolled oats
1/2 cup firmly packed light-brown
  sugar
3 teaspoons baking powder
1/2 teaspoon salt

1 cup milk
1 egg, lightly beaten
4 tablespoons melted butter
1 teaspoon vanilla
3/4 cup raisins
1/2 cup sunflower seeds

Directions:

   Heat oven to 400°. In a large bowl, stir together the flour, oats, brown sugar, baking powder, and salt. In another bowl, blend together the milk, egg, butter, and vanilla. Make a well in the center of the dry ingredients. Add the milk mixture and stir just to combine. Stir in the raisins and sunflower seeds. Fill greased muffin tins. Bake 20 to 22 minutes, or until a tester comes out clean. Cool. Makes one dozen muffins.

Armenian Apricot

2 tablespoons finely chopped dried apricots

5 teaspoons rose water

2 cups minus 2 tablespoons all-purpose flour

1 tablespoon baking powder

1/4 teaspoon salt

1/2 cup granulated sugar

1 cup canned apricots, coarsely chopped (save the juice)

1/3 cup melted butter

1/2 cup milk

1 egg

Directions:

Heat oven to 400°. Soak the finely chopped dried apricots in a mixture of 3 teaspoons rose water and one tablespoon tap water for 20 minutes. In a large bowl, sift together the flour, baking powder, salt, and sugar. In another bowl, combine the melted butter, milk, egg, 1/3 cup of the apricot juice from the canned apricots, and 2 teaspoons of rose water. Strain the dried apricots.

Make a well in the center of the dry ingredients. Pour in the milk mixture, the chopped canned apricots, and the finely chopped dried apricots. Stir just until blended. Fill greased muffin tins. Bake 20 minutes or until the muffins are brown and a tester inserted into the center comes out clean. Cool. Makes one dozen muffins.

The lusciousness of these muffins is intensified by fragrant rose water-- a popular flavoring in Armenian cooking.

Armenian Bulgur

2/3 cup bulgur
1 tablespoon lemon juice
1 (6 ounce) can tomato juice
2 eggs
2 tablespoons olive oil
2 tablespoons corn oil
One minced scallion

1 cup all-purpose flour
2 teaspoons baking powder
1 teaspoon baking soda
1 tablespoon granulated sugar
1/2 teaspoon salt
1 teaspoon cracked pepper
1/2 cup bran flakes

Directions:

Heat oven to 375°. In a small bowl, soak the bulgur in the lemon and tomato juice for 20 minutes. In another bowl, lightly beat the eggs, and then add the olive oil, corn oil, and minced scallion.

Sift together the flour, baking powder, baking soda, sugar, and salt in a large bowl. Stir in the pepper and the bran flakes. Combine the bulgur and the egg mixture. Mix well. Pour the batter into greased muffin tins. Bake for 15 minutes or until the muffins are lightly browned. Makes one dozen muffins.

The nutty flavor of bulgur subtly enhances these exotic Middle Eastern muffins. You can find bulgur in health-food stores and in the bulk food section of some supermarkets.

Anise

2 cups minus 2 tablespoons
  all-purpose flour
1 tablespoon baking powder
1/2 teaspoon salt
1/2 cup granulated sugar
1 egg

1 cup milk
4 tablespoons melted butter
1/4 teaspoon anise extract
1 teaspoon crushed anise seed
1/2 cup raisins
1/2 cup chopped walnuts

Directions:

  Heat oven to 375°. In a large bowl, sift together the flour, baking powder, salt, and sugar. In another bowl, lightly beat the egg. Stir in the milk, melted butter, and anise extract. Pour into the flour mixture. Add the anise seed, raisins, and walnuts. Stir just until moistened.

  Fill greased muffin tins. Bake for 15 minutes or until the muffins are lightly browned. Makes one dozen muffins.

 The subtle licorice flavor enhances these muffins.

Ginger

3 tablespoons fresh gingerroot, peeled
   and grated

3/4 cup light brown sugar

2 tablespoons lemon zest (rind or peel
   from approximately two lemons)

6 tablespoons butter, at room
   temperature

2 eggs

1 cup buttermilk

2 cups all-purpose flour

1/2 teaspoon salt

3/4 teaspoon baking soda

3/4 teaspoon baking powder

1/2 cup gingersnaps

Lemon glaze

1/3 cup lemon juice

1/4 cup granulated sugar

Directions:

   Heat oven to 375°. Coarsely grate the peeled gingerroot to make 3 tablespoons. Cook the ginger and sugar in a small pan over medium heat until the sugar has melted and the mixture is hot. Stir carefully so the sugar does not burn. Remove from the heat and let cool. Add 2 tablespoons finely grated lemon zest to the ginger mixture. In a large mixing bowl, beat together the butter, eggs and buttermilk. In a medium bowl, sift together the flour, salt, baking soda, and baking powder. Add the dry ingredients to the butter mixture and beat until the batter is smooth. Pour in the ginger-lemon mixture and mix well. Crumble the gingersnaps into small pieces and fold into the batter. Spoon the batter into greased muffin tins. Bake 15 minutes or until a tester inserted into the muffins comes out clean. Cool slightly. Pierce the tops and drizzle with lemon glaze. Makes a baker's dozen.

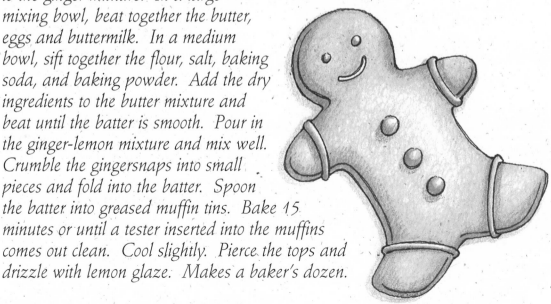

Kiwi Mango

2 ripe kiwis
2 eggs
1/2 cup mango juice
1 teaspoon coconut extract
1/2 cup melted butter

2 cups all-purpose flour
2 teaspoons baking powder
1/2 teaspoon salt
1/2 cup granulated sugar
1/4 cup coconut

Directions:

Heat oven to 350°. Peel the kiwis and slice them into 1/4-inch thick rounds. Set aside. In a medium bowl, whisk together the eggs and mango juice. Stir in the coconut extract and melted butter. In a large bowl, sift together the flour, baking powder, salt, and sugar. Pour the liquid ingredients into the flour mixture. Mix just until the dry ingredients are moistened.

Drop one tablespoon of batter into each greased muffin tin. Place one slice of kiwi on top of the batter and layer with one more tablespoon of batter. Sprinkle with coconut. Bake for 15 to 20 minutes or until a tester inserted into a muffin comes out clean. Makes one dozen muffins.

Note: Bake the muffins on the lower oven rack so that the coconut does not burn.

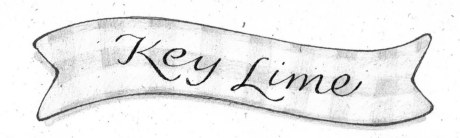

Key Lime

2 cups all-purpose flour
1 teaspoon baking powder
1/4 teaspoon salt
Juice from two limes
Zest from two limes (rind or peel)

3 tablespoons reconstituted lime juice
2 eggs
3/4 cup sweetened condensed milk
4 teaspoons melted butter

Directions:

Heat oven to 350°. In a large bowl sift together the flour, baking powder, and salt. Squeeze the juice from the limes into a medium bowl. Add the lime zest, the reconstituted lime juice, and the eggs. Mix together, lightly beating the eggs. Stir in the sweetened condensed milk and melted butter. Pour into the flour mixture and stir just until moistened.

Fill greased muffin tins. Bake for 15 to 18 minutes or until a tester inserted into a muffin comes out clean. Makes one dozen muffins.

Lox & Cream Cheese

2 cups all-purpose flour
1 tablespoon baking powder
1/8 teaspoon salt
3/4 teaspoon cracked pepper
1 egg
4 tablespoons melted butter
2 tablespoons chopped onion
1 cup milk
1/2 cup chopped lox
   (smoked salmon)

Topping
1/2 cup cream cheese
1 tablespoon milk
2 teaspoons minced onion
2 teaspoons chopped lox

Directions:

Heat oven to 375°. In a large bowl, sift together the flour, baking powder, salt, and pepper. In a small bowl, lightly beat the egg. Add the melted butter, chopped onion, milk, and 1/2 cup chopped lox. Stir the egg mixture into the flour mixture. Fill greased muffin tins.

To make the topping, whip the softened cream cheese with 1 tablespoon milk, and 2 teaspoons each of minced onion and lox. Spread 2 teaspoons of topping over batter in each muffin tin.

Bake for 18 minutes or until done. Makes one dozen muffins. Refrigerate any leftovers.

A unique recipe to serve for brunch that lox lovers will rave about!

Nutmeg

2 cups all-purpose flour
3/4 cup granulated sugar
1 tablespoon baking powder
1 1/2 kernels of nutmeg, grated or 5
    teaspoons of ground nutmeg

1/2 teaspoon salt
1 egg
3/4 cup evaporated milk
3/4 cup whole milk
5 tablespoons melted butter

Directions:

Heat oven to 400°. In a medium bowl, sift together the flour, sugar, baking powder, and salt. Stir in the grated nutmeg. In a small bowl, beat the egg. Add evaporated milk, whole milk, and melted butter. Blend well.

Add the milk mixture to the dry ingredients and stir just until blended. Fill greased muffin tins. Bake for 20 minutes or until the muffin tops are lightly browned. Serve warm. Makes one dozen muffins.

The freshly grated nutmeg makes the flavor of these muffins incomparable!

Mango

3/4 cup whole-wheat flour
3/4 cup sifted all-purpose flour
1/4 cup firmly packed light brown
   sugar
1 teaspoon baking soda
1/4 teaspoon salt
2 eggs

1 cup mashed mango
3 tablespoons corn oil
1/4 cup milk
3 teaspoons dark rum
1/2 teaspoon coconut extract
1/2 teaspoon almond extract

Directions:

   Heat oven to 350°. In a large bowl, mix together the whole-wheat and all-purpose flours, the brown sugar, baking soda, and salt. In a medium bowl, beat the eggs and combine with the mango, corn oil, milk, rum, and coconut and almond extracts. Pour the egg mixture into the flour mixture and stir just until the dry ingredients are moistened.

   Fill greased muffin tins. Bake for 15 to 18 minutes or until a tester inserted into a muffin comes out clean. Makes one dozen muffins.

   Delight your family with the enticing flavors of this summer-time treat from May to September when mangoes are in season.

Mexican Corn

1 1/4 cups sifted all-purpose flour
3/4 cup yellow cornmeal
1/2 rounded teaspoon salt
1 tablespoon baking powder
2 teaspoons granulated sugar

1 (11 ounce) can Green Giant™
   Mexicorn™
1 egg
1 cup milk
1/4 cup corn oil
2 tablespoons chopped scallion greens

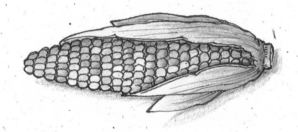

Directions:

Heat oven to 400°. Combine the flour, cornmeal, salt, baking powder, and sugar in a large bowl. Lightly beat the egg in a small bowl; add the milk, corn oil, 2/3 cup Mexicorn™ (from which the liquid has been drained), and the chopped scallion greens. Stir the egg mixture into the flour mixture until the ingredients are blended. Fill greased muffin tins. Bake for 20 to 22 minutes or until a tester comes out clean. Serve warm. Makes one dozen muffins.

Note: These muffins will not brown when they are baked.

Parmesan Tomato

2 cups all-purpose flour
1 tablespoon granulated sugar
1 1/2 teaspoons baking powder
1/2 teaspoon baking soda
1 teaspoon Italian seasoning

3/4 cup Parmesan cheese
1 1/4 cups buttermilk
1/4 cup melted butter
1 egg
1 cup chopped tomato

Directions:

Heat oven to 400°. In a large bowl, sift together the flour, sugar, baking powder, and baking soda. Mix in the Italian seasoning and Parmesan cheese. In a small bowl, mix together the buttermilk, butter, egg, and tomato. Pour the buttermilk mixture into the flour mixture. Stir just until the dry ingredients are moistened. Fill greased muffin tins and bake for 20 minutes or until a tester inserted into a muffin comes out clean. Makes one dozen muffins. Serve warm.

Seafood

2 cups all-purpose flour
1 tablespoon baking powder
1/4 teaspoon salt
1 egg
1 cup crabmeat (use a combination of
canned crab packed in water and
surimi, the crabmeat substitute found
in the seafood section of your grocery
store)

1 1/3 cups milk combined with
liquid from the canned crab
2 tablespoons white wine
Worcestershire sauce
3 tablespoons corn oil
1/2 teaspoon dry mustard
2 tablespoons white cooking wine
6 ounces grated mild cheddar
cheese

Directions:

Heat oven to 375°. In a large bowl, sift together the flour, baking powder, and salt. In a smaller bowl, lightly beat the egg. Drain the crabmeat, saving the liquid. Measure the crabmeat liquid and enough milk to equal 1 1/3 cups. Stir the milk and crabmeat liquid into the egg along with the Worcestershire sauce, corn oil, dry mustard, white wine, and cheese. Mix together. Add the canned crab and surimi. Stir well.

Pour the crabmeat mixture into the flour mixture and stir just until the dry ingredients are moistened. Fill greased muffin tins. Bake for 20 to 25 minutes or until the muffins are lightly browned. Makes one dozen muffins. Refrigerate any leftovers.

Enjoy this muffin with a crisp vegetable salad and a crisp white wine.

Sausage

2 sweet Italian sausages
2 cups all-purpose flour
1 tablespoon baking powder
1/2 teaspoon salt
1/2 cup grated Parmesan cheese

1/8 teaspoon ground pepper
1 teaspoon Italian seasoning
1 egg
1 (15 ounce) jar pizza sauce
3 tablespoons olive oil and/or fat

Directions:

Heat oven to 375°. Remove the sausages from their casing and break into small pieces. Fry them over moderate heat until they are cooked and browned. Drain the sausage on paper towels.

In a large bowl, sift together the flour, baking powder, and salt. Stir in the Parmesan cheese, pepper, and Italian seasoning. In another bowl, lightly beat the egg and blend in the pizza sauce. Add to this mixture enough fat from the sausage plus olive oil to equal 3 tablespoons. Add the sausage and mix well. Pour the pizza sauce mixture into the dry ingredients. Mix just until the ingredients are blended. Fill greased muffin tins. Bake 20 to 25 minutes or until the muffins are firm. Serve warm. Makes one dozen muffins. Refrigerate any leftovers.

Italian sausage and pizza sauce turn an ordinary muffin into a zesty accompaniment for a soup or salad.

Spicy Italian Pizza

1/2 rounded cup chopped tomato

1 teaspoon Italian seasoning

1 teaspoon oregano

2 cups minus 2 tablespoons
   all-purpose flour

1 tablespoon baking powder

1/4 teaspoon salt

1/4 teaspoon minced garlic

1/3 cup pepperoni, diced

1 cup grated mozzarella cheese

1/4 cup Parmesan cheese

1 egg

1 cup milk

5 tablespoons olive oil

Directions:

Heat oven to 400°. In a small bowl, sprinkle the chopped tomato with Italian seasoning and oregano. Set aside. In a large bowl, sift together the flour, baking powder, and salt. Stir in the minced garlic, pepperoni, mozzarella, and Parmesan cheese.

In a medium bowl, lightly beat the egg. Add the milk and olive oil. Pour the milk mixture into the flour mixture and stir well. Fill greased muffin tins. Bake for 15 minutes or until the muffins are lightly browned. Serve warm. Makes one dozen muffins.

Tex-Mex Corn

1 1/4 cups all-purpose flour
3/4 cup yellow cornmeal
1/2 rounded teaspoon salt
1 tablespoon baking powder
1 teaspoon granulated sugar
1 egg

1 cup milk
1/4 cup oil
1 (11-ounce) can GreenGiant™
  Mexicorn™
1 (10 3/4-ounce) can nacho cheese soup
2 tablespoons chopped scallion greens

Directions:

Heat oven to 400°. Combine the flour, cornmeal, salt, baking powder, and sugar in a large bowl. Lightly beat the egg in a small bowl. Add the milk, oil, 3/4 cup Mexicorn™ (from which the liquid has been drained), and cheese soup. Mix well and then add the scallion greens. Add the egg mixture to the flour mixture and stir until the ingredients are blended. Fill greased muffin tins. Bake for 20-22 minutes or until a tester comes out clean. Serve warm. Makes one dozen muffins.

The bold flavor of nacho cheese in these muffins adds a new flavor to cornmeal that will spice up your next barbecue!

Taco

1/2 lb. ground chuck
1/4 cup onion, minced
1/2 package taco seasoning mix
2 cups all-purpose flour
1 1/2 teaspoons baking powder
1/2 teaspoons baking soda
1/2 teaspoon salt
1 (8 oz.) carton sour cream

1/2 cup salsa
1 egg, lightly beaten
1/4 cup milk
4 tablespoons meat drippings or a
   combination of meat drippings
   and corn oil to equal 4 tablespoons
1 cup shredded cheddar cheese

Directions:

Heat oven to 375°. Brown the ground chuck in a frying pan. Add the onion and cook for 5 minutes. Drain and save the drippings. Stir 1/2 of the taco seasoning package into the meat. Set aside. Meanwhile, in a large bowl, sift together the flour, baking powder, baking soda and salt. In another bowl, blend together the sour cream, salsa, egg, milk, and 4 tablespoons meat drippings. Add the liquid mixture to the flour mixture and stir just to combine. Stir in the meat and cheddar cheese. Fill greased muffin tins. Bake 18 to 20 minutes, or until a tester comes out clean. Cool. Makes one dozen muffins. Refrigerate leftovers.

Mincemeat

2 cups all-purpose flour
1/3 cup sugar
2 teaspoons baking powder
1/2 teaspoon salt
1 1/4 cups prepared mincemeat

2 eggs, lightly beaten
1/3 cup milk
1/3 cup corn oil
1 teaspoon vanilla
1 cup chopped walnuts

Directions:

   Heat oven to 350°. In a large bowl, stir together the flour, sugar, baking powder, and salt. In another bowl, blend together the mincemeat, eggs, milk, oil and vanilla. Make a well in the center of the dry ingredients. Add the mincemeat mixture and stir just to combine. Stir in the walnuts. Fill greased muffin tins. Bake 18 to 20 minutes, or until a tester comes out clean. Cool. Makes one dozen muffins.

INDEX

Waiting for the completion of Dot Vartan's second book
is much like opening the door to a home filled with
the aromas of a delectable vegetable stock simmering on the stove…
oh, the anticipation! Wait no longer—the soup is done!
The perfect companion to Dot's first book, *Mad About Muffins*,
this publication is full of the freshest formulas for every soup imaginable.
Featuring a soup for every season, *Is It Soup Yet?* belongs in every kitchen.

To order *Is It Soup Yet?* call 1-800-377-3566. Among Friends offers other cookbooks,
including their classics, *Just a Matter of Thyme* and *With Heart & Soul*.
Please allow us to give you the name of a retail store in your area.

THE AMONG FRIENDS LIBRARY